THE BLENDED
HOME

A HOLISTIC GUIDE TO HAPPINESS &
HARMONY FOR YOUR BLENDED FAMILY

KAREN BROWNING

Key Vitality Publishing

Cover design by Dawn Moore
Author image by Randy Parietti
ISBN (paperback): 979-8-9994808-0-4
ISBN (ebook): 979-8-9994808-1-1
ISBN (audiobook): 979-8-9994808-1-1
Library of Congress Control Number: 2025916904

For permissions or inquiries, contact customersuccess@keyvitality.org
Visit www.keyvitality.org for more resources on creating harmonious blended homes.

First Edition, December 2025
Printed in the United States of America

Published in the United States by: Key Vitality Publishing

CONTENTS

Dedication   V

Preface   VI

Introduction   VIII

1. Designing Spaces That Bring People Together   1

2. Decluttering for Connection   9

3. Clearing Emotional Energy   19

4. The Morning Flow to Start the Day   27

5. The Family Room Reset   35

6. The Bedroom as a Sanctuary   43

7. The Kitchen Connection   53

8. Creating Positive Rituals   61

9. Bridging Differences with Shared Goals   69

10. The Power of Energetic Boundaries   77

11. From Chaos to Calm with Mindset Shifts   85

12. Manifesting the Path Forward   93

13. Your Bonus   103

Conclusion   106

Acknowledgements   107

About the author   108

I dedicate this book with much love and gratitude to my own blended family, my clients, and to all others who have supported me on my journey to help transform one household at a time. This book is as much yours as it is mine.

PREFACE

WHY THE BLENDED HOME IS DIFFERENT

"Your home is not just a place; it's an extension of your energy. Align it with your vision, and it will support your dreams."
—Unknown

If you've ever read Marie Kondo's *The Life-Changing Magic of Tidying Up*, you know the power of decluttering to spark joy. Or perhaps books like *The 7 Habits of Highly Effective Families* have inspired stronger family bonds. While these works offer timeless wisdom, *The Blended Home* carves a unique path for blended families seeking harmony in their shared spaces and hearts.

Unlike decluttering guides that focus solely on physical spaces, this book weaves ancient Feng Shui principles with modern life coaching strategies to transform both your home's energy and your family's dynamics. Where general family coaching books provide broad advice, my approach is tailored to the intricate balance of blended families—merging households with grace. Drawing from my journey as a bonus mom and creator of the transformational program *The Blended Circle*, I offer a holistic roadmap to create a home where everyone feels seen and valued.

The purpose of this book is to equip blended families with tools to achieve:

- **A peaceful and connected home:** Using Feng Shui principles, create a supportive, balanced, and calming haven for all.

- **Stronger family bonds:** With coaching techniques, gain tools to improve communication, resolve conflicts, and build deeper connections.

- **Clarity and confidence:** Whether a biological or bonus parent, feel confident leading with love and intention.

- **Emotional resilience:** Learn to manage emotions, avoid burnout, and stay grounded amid family challenges.

- **Hope and possibility:** Thrive; don't just survive. Feel hopeful, equipped with tools for lasting harmony.

From redesigning rooms that foster unity to setting energetic boundaries that honor individual needs, *The Blended Home* supplies you with practical strategies and soulful insights. Whether you're a stepparent, co-parent, or family member blending new traditions, this book is your guide to crafting a sanctuary of love and connection. Join me to discover a path that is uniquely yours.

INTRODUCTION

HOW TO CREATE HAPPINESS AND HARMONY IN YOUR BLENDED FAMILY

"Where we love is home—home that our feet may leave, but not our hearts."
— Oliver Wendell Holmes

I am not sure whether it was a near-death experience—I don't believe I died—but I've always wondered. The early morning was bitterly cold, though I didn't feel it. Not yet. When I woke, my head rested on the steering wheel, uncertain if I'd stirred on impact or moments later. Brushing aside what I thought was hair, I felt sticky warmth. Blood coated my fingers, droplets sliding down my forehead, pooling on my face and neck. The sight was surreal, yet the world was eerily quiet. Questions about survival and purpose stirred in my mind.

Earlier that evening, I'd been hanging out with friends, back home for college break. I was the designated driver, dropping each person off. At the last stop, my buddy wanted to talk about his girlfriend troubles. Sitting in my car with the engine idling, we talked through his heartbreak. Minutes turned into hours, and the clock hit 2 a.m.

"You're exhausted," I said, urging him to chat another day. I needed to get home. My parents' house was 20 minutes away. I could stay awake for that, couldn't I?

Turns out I couldn't. My eyes closed for a moment too long, and I crashed into a light pole. My car was totaled. Over a hundred stitches in my head, a broken ankle, and a collapsed lung—it was a miracle I was alive. There were no airbags back then, but I wore a seatbelt, which likely saved me. Or maybe it was something else entirely. That night, I wasn't alone.

I didn't tell anyone about the voice and the ethereal sense. When asked about the accident, I described the crash and injuries but kept the mystical part to myself. How do you explain something like that?

Unconscious or caught between life and death, I desperately wanted to go home. I thought about it, perhaps saying aloud, "*I just want to go home.*" And then I felt it, a presence that was overwhelming and comforting, like being wrapped in a warm blanket. I existed in the vast darkness of the universe, yet I sensed a brilliant light all around me. The dialogue was strange, both words and a felt sense, happening in my head and beyond.

"*People can have many loving homes,*" the voice said. The light burned brighter as my body ached with a love so pure.

"*Yes,*" I thought. "*That's why I want to go home.*" Did home mean heaven? Was I dying? My thoughts scrambled, yet I was oddly at peace.

The presence continued: "*Show them how.*" It was more of a full-body understanding than a faint whisper because even now it's hard to describe in words. I felt the significance of a grander purpose.

And just as quickly, the warmth was gone, the light returned to nighttime, and the voice vanished. I was back in my car, blinking through blood and pain, realizing the enormity of what had just happened.

For years, I kept that moment private. It didn't make sense, and I didn't want people to think I was crazy. I dismissed it as imagination or the rush of adrenaline, burying the memory deep.

Then I met my husband. When he told me he had two kids, my logical brain hesitated. Dating someone with kids felt daunting, especially when I was still looking for fairytale love. Then I heard it again, as clear as the night of the accident: "*People can have many loving homes. Show them how.*"

That voice had guided me through years of growth, and now I realized its purpose: to help others build loving homes.

Through practical steps, you too can transform your home into a sanctuary of connection. This book blends Feng Shui—the ancient practice of balancing energy in your home—with life coaching to shift your mindset and navigate family dynamics with confidence and clarity.

You'll learn how to:

- Design spaces that naturally bring people together and reduce conflict;

- Clear clutter to release emotional weight and foster relationships;

- Set energetic and emotional boundaries to promote balance;

- Create peaceful routines and rituals for stability and connection;

- Use manifestation to build a shared vision for your family's future.

Step by step, this book will guide you in aligning your home's energy with your family's vision for love and connection. You don't need to be a Feng Shui expert or change who you are. Small, intentional changes yield big results.

I'm not just offering theories—I've lived these principles. As a bonus mom for over a decade, I know the struggles and joys of blending a family. As a certified Feng Shui practitioner and life coach, I've helped people create harmony in their homes and lives. My background in communication and higher education adds a practical edge to my approach.

This journey unfolds in three parts: First, we'll redesign your physical spaces to foster connection. Next, we'll clear emotional barriers to build stronger bonds. Finally, we'll create routines and mindsets for lasting harmony. Each chapter offers action-oriented practices to bring your blended family closer. Throughout this book, you'll find 'Reflect and Record Your Progress' prompts to deepen your journey. Use a notebook, digital device, or any method that feels right to capture your insights and track your family's transformation.

This book isn't about perfection; it's about progress. Through my stories, client successes, Feng Shui principles, and life coaching tools, you'll find inspiration to help you transform your blended family. Guided by a voice that taught me people can have many loving homes, I've written this book to empower you to move from limitations to possibilities. If I can create a peaceful sanctuary, so can you. Let's build your loving home together.

Chapter 1

DESIGNING SPACES THAT BRING PEOPLE TOGETHER

HOW INTENTIONAL DESIGNS CULTIVATE POSITIVE CONNECTIONS

"The best rooms have something to say about the people who live in them."

—David Hicks

D esigning a space is like setting a table for a feast, each choice an invitation to connect. You choose the tablecloth that softens the surface, the lighting that creates the ambience, and the arrangement of chairs that encourages eye contact and easy conversation. The power of design is subtle but transformative. It says, *"You belong here. There's a place for you at this table."* In a blended family, people come with different histories, preferences, and emotional ingredients. You can't always predict how everyone will show up, but you can prepare the space to welcome them fully. And over time, with shared meals, stories, and laughter layered into the intentionally designed space, it becomes a gathering place for hearts.

Tarek El Moussa and Christina Haack—the stars of HGTV's *Flip or Flop* and competitors on *The Flip Off*—embody this intentionality. Originally, they were a married couple with two kids, known for transforming rundown properties into dream homes. Their differences in design styles, budgeting, and overall approach to flipping houses often resulted in heated, yet entertaining, moments. In one memorable episode, Christina picked out an expensive backsplash, much to Tarek's dismay, and they argued over whether it was a "statement piece" or an unnecessary splurge. Though divorced, they continue working together, merging business, home design, and co-parenting into a functional, if sometimes challenging, dynamic. They had to navigate boundaries, communication struggles, and shifting roles, but through it all, they remained focused on their shared goals: raising their children and maintaining a thriving business. Their experience perfectly parallels the world of blended families, where balancing differences while working toward an agreeable shared vision is key.

In this chapter, you'll learn how to design spaces that unite your blended family using life coaching to guide intention and Feng Shui to align energy. These tools will transform your home into a gathering place for love, balance, and connection, setting the foundation for a harmonious journey.

Why intentional design matters

Your home is a container for your family's energy, shaping interactions and emotions. The way a space is designed can either encourage connection or create subtle barriers that keep people apart. Feng Shui teaches that chi—life force energy—flows smoothly in balanced environments, fostering harmony. When energy gets stuck, whether through poor layout, clutter, or harsh design choices, it can amplify tension and conflict.

Merging two families under one roof comes with its own unique set of challenges. Different backgrounds, traditions, and personal styles can sometimes feel like they're clashing rather than complementing each other. One partner may favor minimalism, another cozy eclecticism. Kids may crave personal space while parents seek shared areas. One parent may prefer structure and routine, while the other embraces flexibility and spontaneity. These differences can spark conflict, leaving the home feeling "off."

When you intentionally design a space with connection in mind, you create an environment for better communication, deeper bonds, and lasting harmony—far beyond mere furniture. Life coaching rituals, like family design meetings, unify shared visions. Feng Shui principles—open pathways, warm lighting—align chi, fostering welcoming spaces. Just as a thoughtfully set table invites guests to gather and savor a meal, this intentionality encourages blended family members to merge with ease. Such choices transform a house into a home where connection thrives, not by chance but by intention. When your home's energy mirrors your family's, magic unfolds.

A worldwide look back

Cultures have long designed spaces to foster connection, offering wisdom for blended families. These layouts unified families, much like in today's homes.

In traditional Chinese architecture, the *siheyuan*—a courtyard-style home—was structured so that all rooms faced inward to promote a stronger vibration of unity and communication. The placement of doors, furniture, and communal spaces followed Feng Shui guidelines to optimize energy flow and ensure balance within the household. This approach highlights how intentional space design can encourage positive interactions and emotional well-being, which is a valuable lesson for blended families seeking to create a sense of unity.

In medieval European homes, where castles and manors were often divided into private quarters, the great hall remained a central space for shared meals, discussions, and celebrations. This communal space symbolized unity within the household, reinforcing that despite the existence of individual rooms and separate personal spaces, the family was still a collective unit. Today, blended families can adopt this concept by designating shared areas in the home specific to conversation and quality time.

Across time periods and cultures, one truth remains constant: the design of a home shapes the relationships within it. For blended families, understanding these historical approaches can inspire modern day design choices that create a true sense of home for everyone.

The energy behind intentional design

My own inspired design choices taught me the power of intentionality. The kitchen is often called the heart of the home—but during our remodel, it felt more like the center of chaos than connection. What started as a dream to create a more functional and welcoming space for our blended family quickly spiraled into dust, decisions, and disconnection.

While the work was being done, we relocated to the basement, eating meals around a wobbly fold-out table. Because of the awkward layout, we all sat on one side—lined up like panelists at a press conference. Conversations felt stiff and strained. Small annoyances turned into bigger ones, and beneath the remodeling stress, I sensed something deeper: our space was working against us.

As a Feng Shui practitioner, I knew better than to dismiss it. Our surroundings shape our energy and our interactions. Physical layout isn't just about aesthetics; it communicates what kind of engagement is invited. Sitting side by side, without the ability to face each other, created an invisible wall between us.

When the remodel was finished, we were excited to move back upstairs. But as soon as we sat at the beautiful new island, I realized we had unintentionally recreated the same problem. All the seating was on one side again. Conversations stalled. The space felt... off. Even my husband, who had resisted more changes, admitted something didn't feel quite right.

Trusting my instincts, we made adjustments. We added seating on both sides of the island, introduced softer lighting, and cleared surfaces of unnecessary clutter. The shift was immediate. Conversations began to flow again. People lingered longer. The space, once strained, now felt alive, balanced, and welcoming.

This experience reaffirmed what I teach in both life coaching and Feng Shui: your home's design has a profound effect on your family's energy and connection. It's not about a flawless kitchen or an expensive remodel—it's about choosing elements, layouts, and objects that support your intention. Whether it's a $5 lamp or a new seating arrangement, when your space is aligned with your desire for connection, your home becomes a container for it.

The takeaway is simple: when the energy of your home supports your goals, your relationships shift too. You don't need more space or a perfect space—you need more intention.

The science of intentional design

Research shows that environments shape relationships, and healthy relationships are vital for blended families seeking unity.

- **Organized spaces ease stress.**[1] Research in the *Journal of Environmental Psychology* shows organized layouts lower stress levels, fostering emotional clarity. A tidy home creates a calm environment, uniting blended families in stability.

- **Nature boosts well-being.**[2] Studies on biophilic design (bringing nature indoors) from *Building and Environment* find that plants, natural textures, and fresh air reduce anxiety, depression, and fatigue by raising serotonin levels. Greenery in shared spaces soothes stepfamily tensions.

- **Emotions shape energy.**[3] Research on emotional contagion from the journal *Emotion* reveals that energy in a space is influenced by the emotions of those who inhabit it. Resetting spaces with positive intentions influences how people feel and interact within blended homes.

- **Layout drives connection.**[4] According to an *Environment and Behavior* study, the layout and design of shared spaces impact communication, cooperation, and emotional connection. Cramped environments or poorly arranged spaces spark tension—even if people aren't consciously aware of it.

These findings highlight how intentional design acts as a connection-creator for nurturing harmony. Let's explore practical steps to shape it.

How to design intentionally

Designing for connection blends life coaching practices with Feng Shui's energy alignment, creating a welcoming space for your blended family. These steps, which can be done in any order, foster unity and warmth, nurturing spaces where love prospers:

1. **Arrange seating for connection:** Angle chairs inward in shared spaces (e.g., living rooms, nooks) to spark conversation, encouraging unity among family members. Avoid linear setups that create physical and emotional distance.

2. **Choose warm lighting:** Install dimmable lamps or warm bulbs in common areas to create coziness. Adjust lighting nightly during meals to foster relaxed, open conversations, along with emotional warmth.

3. **Use round or oval tables:** Opt for shapes that promote equality, ensuring everyone feels included in conversations. For rectangular tables, add a circular centerpiece to draw energy inward and balance the space.

4. **Clear the clutter:** Keep surfaces like floors and table-tops tidy to allow chi to flow freely. Declutter weekly, removing non-essentials, to reduce stress and create space for clarity and connection.

5. **Personalize the space:** Add photos, artwork, or meaningful objects that reflect your family's personality to build a sense of belonging. Ensure all members contribute a memento or personal portrait to feel included.

6. **Place mirrors for prosperity:** Position a mirror near the dining table to "double" food, symbolizing abundance. This enhances energetic flow, boosting family and financial prosperity, helping the household to flourish.

These small shifts—from seating placement to lighting choices—transform how your blended family interacts, weaving harmony into every ingredient of your home.

Client Case Study

One of my clients called me in because her blended family was struggling with health and mindset challenges, along with disconnection with both immediate and extended family. Annoyances seemed to fester, which resulted in passive-aggressive arguments, or at other times, communication was practically nonexistent. Once I arrived at their home, it didn't take long for me to see one of the core issues: the dining table was completely buried under piles of stuff. The table wasn't just covered with paperwork and toys; it had quietly become a storage space rather than a gathering place. The clutter stretched into nearby areas, creating an unintentional block between family members.

My client's family wasn't using the table for its intended purpose. Instead, they ate every meal on trays in the living room, facing the TV, which was draining the energy. It was no wonder the family wasn't in harmony. Eating while facing the TV disconnected them from one another, along with the clutter on the table blocking the flow of chi throughout their home—something we'll dive into more deeply in the next chapter.

In Feng Shui, the dining table symbolizes family unity, nourishment, and abundance; it's a key area for every family's prosperity. Keeping the table clutter-free, well-lit, and inviting not only strengthens relationships but also attracts wealth, good health, and positive energy into a home. Once I explained how this setup was impacting their blended family dynamics, they cleared the table and made it a priority to eat meals together at the dining table. The transformation was incredible. When she checked in a few weeks later, after the rest of the clutter had been cleared, she told me, *"It's like magic. We're actually talking to each other now, even my stepchildren! Everyone feels more connected, and I even feel a new spark with my husband that I haven't felt in years."*

What seemed like a simple change—clearing the table and reclaiming it as a space to gather—had a profound ripple effect. Within a month, mealtime became a consistent point of connection, and the family even began hosting extended relatives again, something they hadn't done in over two years. Facing each other also created a space that invited connection, conversation, and closeness. This shift shows blended families that intentional design fosters unity, transforming spaces into havens of love. Start with some simple intentional steps on your way to big changes in your family's connection.

Did You Know?

- *Sitting face to face encourages conversation and connection, while sitting side by side can reduce eye contact and engagement.*

- *Poor lighting—either too dim or overly harsh—can increase stress levels, while warm, natural light fosters relaxation and positivity.*

- *Circular seating arrangements help everyone feel included, avoiding the hierarchy often created by rectangular tables.*

- *Families who collaborate on home design decisions experience a stronger sense of unity and shared purpose.*

Your Turn

Your home is a feast table; it's designed as an invitation for gathering and connection. Each reflective step sets a place for your blended family, cultivating harmony with purpose and care.

Mantra: "*When I design space with intention, I invite harmony into my home.*" Keep this mantra in mind as you try these steps in any order, allowing it to guide your actions and intentions.

1. **Assess your table:** Ask yourself, is the table clear and inviting? If not, remove anything that doesn't belong. Keep the surface free for meals and family time. Add a centerpiece, like a small plant or candle, to anchor the energy and make the space feel intentional. How does it look and feel now?

2. **Rearrange the seating:** Is the seating arranged to facilitate eye contact and conversation? Balance the energy by encouraging interaction and connection with a new arrangement. In what ways can I better align my home's energy with my family goals?

3. **Set the mood with lighting:** Does the lighting feel warm and welcoming, or harsh and uninviting? Add a lamp, dimmer switch, or candles to create a cozy atmosphere. Or switch to a less bright bulb. How does the mood shift?

4. **Make it a ritual:** What energy does my home currently hold, and how does it impact my emotions? Commit to eating together at the dining table for at least three meals a week. Observe how the energy in the space and in your family shifts. What changes happened in your blended family's connection?

Reflect and Record Your Progress: After one week of design shifts, write down one or more positive changes in your home's energy or family interactions (e.g., "*We talked more at dinner*"). How does the space feel? What new bonds are forming? How can this feast table become the heart of your family?

Let each design choice be an invitation to deepen authenticity. Your home is a canvas for connection—its energy shaped by design. Every day is an opportunity to choose harmony, connection, and a home filled with positive energy where love thrives.

Chapter 2

DECLUTTERING FOR CONNECTION

How Clearing Clutter Fosters Stronger Family Bonds

"Out of clutter, find simplicity. From discord, find harmony."
—Albert Einstein

Decluttering is like tending to a family garden. At first, a few weeds—piles of mail, scattered toys—seem harmless. But over time, they multiply, crowding out the space meant for connection and calm. In blended families, these weeds often sprout from merged lives, blocking the chi that fosters harmony. Clearing them creates a home where love can bloom.

In blended households, clutter often reflects the fusing of families—past homes, different parenting styles, and memories. Each time you release something, it lightens your home and heart, freeing emotional weight and making room for what truly matters. Decluttering is a shared act of renewal and can be viewed as planting seeds of growth.

Karen's home, featured on the television show *Hoarders*, was chaotic. Yellowed magazines were stacked up to the ceiling, while towers of boxes spilled their contents onto the floor. The dining table was buried under clutter: unopened mail, broken mugs, and random odds and ends. Every step echoed the tension that had built up over years of neglect.

Karen stood in the doorway, arms crossed tightly with embarrassment and defeat. *"It's just stuff,"* she whispered, her voice barely betraying the truth. But it wasn't just stuff. The clutter was a physical manifestation of emotional weight. The home's silence reflected disconnectedness. Her kids rarely visited, and when they did, conversations were strained. The chaos mirrored their distance.

But as they decluttered, the atmosphere shifted. Each piece that was removed began to lift the heaviness that had settled over the house. Karen watched as her table emerged, its surface scratched but sturdy. Tears welled: "*We used to sit here for hours,*" she whispered, "*I didn't realize how much I missed that.*" Then with tears in her eyes, Karen's daughter spoke: "*We can finally sit together and talk again, Mom.*"

When the family gathered around that table again, conversation flowed, laughter replaced awkward silences, and Karen felt hope. Clearing the space hadn't just also transformed her home—it had reconnected her family.

Karen's story reflects our own. Our homes hold our energy, and when it becomes stuck, it keeps us from moving forward. With purpose, we can release what no longer serves us and create spaces where connection and joy thrive.

Why decluttering matters

Like weeds in a garden, clutter takes over, crowding out the beauty you're trying to cultivate. Clutter is stagnant energy, and it blocks connection and harmony. In Feng Shui, clutter represents indecision, overwhelm, and unfinished business, disrupting the flow of chi. A chaotic space fuels chaotic interaction, whether you're a stepparent, co-parent, or new family member navigating blended dynamics.

Blended families face unique clutter challenges. Each member brings history, habits, and belongings, which pile up both physically and emotionally. Shared spaces can feel overwhelming as everyone finds a place, both figuratively and literally. Clutter symbolizes unresolved conflicts or competing priorities. Imagine a hutch filled with items from separate lives. It's a visual reminder of the blending challenges of blending lives. These piles can amplify feelings of disconnection, as if the home struggles to find unity.

Communal clutter exposes deeper differences in parenting styles, reflecting conflicting values, expectations, or emotional triggers. One parent might see clutter as chaos that needs to be controlled, while another views it as normal family life. Messy areas might highlight favoritism, uneven responsibilities, or unspoken rules, which spark frustration and resentment. A pile of schoolwork or toys strewn about the living room symbolizes struggles over boundaries, control, and belonging. For children in blended families, clutter can unintentionally amplify feelings of overwhelm or displacement.

Here's the good news: decluttering creates intentional spaces for connection, peace, and happiness. Clearing the excess creates room for relationships and memories that matter most. A clutter-free space invites in meaningful moments like shared meals, conversations, and a sense of belonging. For children, creating open, welcoming areas helps them feel at home.

For blended families, decluttering is deeply symbolic. Clearing shared spaces sends a powerful message: *"This is our home now."* It's not about erasing the past, but rather, making room for a shared future. Decluttering is an act of unity, saying, *"We're in this together."* Merging households often means combining possessions from different lives. Involve all family members in choosing what stays, ensuring everyone's voice is heard. For example, let stepchildren pick one item to display in a shared space, symbolizing their place in the home. Like a family garden, clearing clutter welcomes space for children and adults alike to flourish in their new blended environment. Tidying up creates freedom for relationships to blossom and grow stronger.

A worldwide look back

The idea that clutter impacts our well-being isn't new. Throughout history, cultures around the world have understood the importance of creating planned, uncluttered spaces to support harmony and balance.

In ancient Japan, minimalism shaped homes. The concept of *ma*, or empty space, was both a design choice and a philosophy. Every open corner and carefully placed piece of furniture guided the ki (the Japanese life force energy, akin to chi) to flow freely, promoting stability and balance. This "breathing room" fostered peace, both aesthetically and spiritually, so relationships could thrive.

In the mid-20th century, the "open concept" movement began to emerge, valuing simplicity and functionality. Post-war homes embraced clean lines, open layouts, and natural light. The shift wasn't just about style, though; it reflected a desire to connect more deeply with family and simplify life after years of global upheaval.

These historical trends remind us of an important truth: the way we maintain our spaces has always been a mirror of our emotional lives, and clutter-free spaces nurture connection by letting energy flow. Today, we can elicit inspiration from the past and reclaim the soul of our homes.

The energy behind decluttering

Decluttering transformed my blended family. Before I earned my Feng Shui certification, I studied as a professional organizer. I loved tidying but felt something was missing. I realized decluttering wasn't just about organizing objects; it was about aligning a home's energy with balanced harmony. Clutter produces stagnant energy, amplifying tension and disconnection. Clearing clutter removes emotional and energetic blocks, inviting connection into the home and relationships.

This lesson hit home after my stepsons returned from a transformative trip to Africa. They went to help build a dormitory for Kenyan girls who lived with few possessions. They treasured their belongings, as if each item were priceless. My stepsons were struck by how little the girls had, yet how happy and connected they were. "*We have so much stuff we don't even use or need,*" one said on the flight home.

Their perspective then shifted. The overflowing closets and gadgets cluttering their room seemed less important. Inspired by the simplicity and joy they had witnessed, they cleared out what was no longer needed and donated bags of clothes, toys, and games to charities. "*It feels lighter in here,*" my youngest stepson said. He was right, the room felt physically lighter, like a dark weighted blanket had been lifted.

My daughter also noticed the negative impact of clutter. She struggled with nightmares and restless sleep for months. Her mood grew cranky, and her energy dipped. I couldn't fathom why sleep was so elusive. Studying Feng Shui revealed the issue: her bed had drawers underneath, filled with toys, trinkets, and miscellaneous items. In Feng Shui, energy must flow freely around a bed for restful sleep. Cluttered areas underneath create stagnation, disrupting peace and relaxation.

I cleared the drawers, removing everything. The change was remarkable; her nightmares stopped! She slept soundly and woke happy, well-rested, and ready for the day. The return of her smile and energy moved me deeply. This was concrete proof that physical clutter directly affects our well-being.

If space limitations mean you must store items under your bed, try restricting this to soft items like bedding and linens. These allow energy to flow freely, maintaining a calm environment. Avoid rigid, hard, or bulky items that block the flowing chi. Everyone in your blended family deserves a harmonious home. Decluttering sends a powerful message: "*This is our fresh start.*"

The science of decluttering

Decluttering isn't about forcing changes around messy habits. Rather, research demonstrates that our environment shapes stress, mental function, and emotional well-being to support a happier home.

- **Clutter raises stress.**[5] A study in the *Journal of Personality and Social Psychology* shows cluttered spaces increase cortisol. The brain struggles to filter distractions, causing mental fatigue, irritability, and mental strain. Clearing clutter in blended family homes restores calm and emotional resilience.

- **Decluttering enhances clarity.**[6] According to a study from *Personality and Social Psychology Bulletin*, cluttered homes bring more fatigue and depression than restful spaces. A tidy home promotes peace, easing anxiety and boosting blended family harmony.

- **Clutter clouds focus.**[7] Research from the *Journal of Neuroscience* reveals clutter overwhelms the brain's processing capacity, making it harder to focus and be present. A clear space helps blended families stay engaged and connected.

- **Clutter affects children.**[8] Research from *Developmental Psychology* demonstrates that kids in cluttered spaces struggle with concentration and managing emotions. Decluttering supports children in blended families with clarity, focus, and emotional regulation.

Like weeds choking a garden, clutter drains energy. Clearing it frees space for connection and calm. Now that we've seen clutter's effects, let's create a home that fosters connection with these steps.

How to declutter for connection

Decluttering is often seen as a chore, reflecting struggles to mix traditions and belongings. However, in blended families, decluttering can build togetherness and create a home that belongs to everyone. Try these steps:

1. **Choose a starting point:** Identify one cluttered area that feels consuming, such as the dining table, kitchen counters, or family room. Remember, start small to avoid feeling overwhelmed; even a single drawer will have a positive and uplifting effect.

2. **Sort and simplify:** Create four piles: keep here, keep elsewhere, donate, and discard. Keep only items that serve a purpose or bring joy. When you're letting go, you're freeing items for a new chapter.

3. **Set boundaries:** Establish rules for shared spaces, like keeping the dining table purely for meals and conversations, free of backpacks, mail, or clutter. Give every item a designated place, fostering a sense of belonging for all.

4. **Create intentional zones:** Use bins, trays, or baskets to organize items and assign them places. These delegated zones prevent clutter from returning. Think of it this way: pilots don't just drop passengers off at any airport—they make sure everyone arrives at their exact destination.

5. **Make it a family effort :** Involve the family, explaining how clutter creates a more peaceful home. Make it fun! Play upbeat music and set a timer for twenty-five minutes with a five-minute break, turning the task into a game.

6. **Enhance the family corner:** According to the Feng Shui Bagua map—where each compass direction denotes a key life area—the East sector of your home represents "family & new beginnings". Clear clutter here to boost family harmony. Also, add greenery (like plants) and family heirlooms to symbolize growth and unity.

SOUTHEAST	SOUTH	SOUTHWEST
Wealth & Prosperity	*Fame & Reputation*	*Love & Relationships*
EAST	CENTER	WEST
Family & New Beginnings	*Health & Well-being*	*Children & Creativity*
NORTHEAST	NORTH	NORTHWEST
Knowledge & Spirituality	*Career & Life's Journey*	*Travel & Helpful People*

Classical Feng Shui Bagua Map

Decluttering helps blended families establish balance as a shared household. Each step brings people closer to happiness and harmony. Your home will reflect your new unified front.

Client Case Study

A specialty hair salon owner hired me. Her salon focused on clients with hair loss—often cancer patients—offering custom hairpieces to restore dignity and confidence. This work was deeply meaningful, but the shop still felt heavy.

When I first met my client, I was overwhelmed by the clutter in her shop. The retail section overflowed with inventory, and surfaces were covered with gifts from clients: dusty stuffed animals, oversized plants crowding corners, and dried flowers scattered everywhere. The energy felt heavy and stagnant, despite the kindness behind these gifts.

Assessing the space, I asked about the clutter. She said every item held sentimental value from cherished clients, making it hard to part with them. As we talked, I noticed holding onto these objects stifled her, much like many of the blended families I work with. Gifts of gratitude from past chapters that had now been converted to stagnant energy, blocking the present and future. Spaces—whether they are salons, offices, or a blended family home—can all hold "gifts of the past" that no longer serve the present.

Next, we acknowledged each item's role and released what didn't serve her shop. The energy began to shift. I performed an energetic cleansing with chimes, sage, and set intentions. (I'll share more on energetic cleansing in Chapter 3.) Her retail section then became open and inviting, and the salon area became a calming client space.

Afterward, she shared the following:

"After finding Karen accidentally, we started the work together. My instincts told me that Karen was very humble, and her approach was with loving energy. She provided a consultation, and the first Feng Shui application to help the energy in my business space has been very impressive. A true burden-lifting experience has occurred, and I actually feel residual negative energies have been removed. I have people proclaiming they feel so good coming into my shop. They describe it as calming and nurturing. Those adjectives are worth a million to me since I help cancer patients full time with the services I provide."

In the months that followed, she reported an increased number of client referrals, and because of the response from her clients, I go back annually to complete the space-clearing process. This transformation wasn't just about a visually appealing space. It aligned the shop with her mission, offering hope and care for a compassionate future.

> *Did You Know?*
> - *Organized spaces promote faster sleep and fewer nightly disturbances, allowing for a better night's sleep.*
>
> - *Chaotic spaces promote stressful eating and poor food choices, contributing to unhealthy dietary habits.*
>
> - *Tables covered in clutter discourage shared experiences and meaningful conversations.*

Your Turn

Decluttering can feel manageable. Start small and stay consistent. And watch as your space and family's dynamics transform as you follow these steps.

Mantra: "*When I clear clutter, I create clarity and ease.*" Notice how physical and mental space opens as you make intentional choices.

1. **Assess emotional attachments:** Note how clutter makes you feel—stressed, nostalgic, guilty, or overwhelmed? Identify items tied to heavy emotions.

2. **Reflect on family energy:** Analyze your shared spaces: are they open and welcoming, or heavy and chaotic? Consider how clutter impacts your family's mood.

3. **Visualize and set intentions:** Imagine your home without excess items. How does it make you feel? Replace "*I must clean*" with "*I am creating a peaceful and inviting home.*" What intentional words resonate with you?

4. **Create a gratitude ritual:** Rather than keeping clutter out of obligation, thank each item before letting it go. Schedule weekly fifteen-minute family declutter sessions with music and a shared snack. How does this ritual reframe clutter and shift your family's connection?

Reflect and Record Your Progress: After a week or two of decluttering, write down one or more positive changes in your home's energy or family dynamics (e.g., *"The kitchen feels peaceful, and we're talking more"*). Have family interactions improved? How does this motivate you to continue?

Your clutter-free home is a foundation for harmony. Consistency matters: a few minutes each day shapes the space where connection and joy flourish. Forget perfection; it's about progress. Every step creates a home of love and freedom—like a beautiful family garden.

Chapter 3

CLEARING EMOTIONAL ENERGY

HOW TO RELEASE "STUCK" ENERGY TO FOSTER FAMILY HARMONY

"Energy cannot be created or destroyed, it can only be changed from one form to another."
—Albert Einstein

C learing emotional energy is like opening your front door after a long, stormy winter. The air in your home grows thick with the weight of unspoken words, lingering sadness, or the echoes of past arguments. You might not notice at first, adjusting to the heavy atmosphere as you navigate daily life. But then, you fling open the window, and crisp air rushes in, stirring dust in forgotten corners and coaxing the curtains to dance. The house breathes again, alive with possibility. In blended families, where emotions from different histories swirl like storm clouds, clearing this energy releases old tensions and invites peace. It's a quiet but powerful act, telling your home, *"The past no longer owns this space. We're ready for a fresh start."*

Alicia Keys and Swizz Beatz faced their own storm in their blended family. When Alicia entered Swizz's life, his previous marriage left a trail of hurt feelings and misunderstandings. Co-parenting with Swizz's ex-wife, Mashonda, was fraught with tension—miscommunications piled up, and old wounds resurfaced, creating a heavy atmosphere for their children. But they chose to clear the air. Through honest conversations, mutual respect, and commitment to their kids, they released resentment and built a vitality of collaboration. Today, they share celebrations, holidays, and vacations, laughing together as a unified family. Their story shows that clearing emotional energy isn't about erasing the past—it's about making room for a brighter present. Your home can become this kind of sanctuary, where love and connection succeed.

In this chapter, you'll learn to spot stuck energy—those heavy, tense feelings in your home—and release them with Feng Shui rituals like smudging and sound cleansing. Paired with life coaching tools for mindset shifts, these practices will help your blended family, despite complex dynamics, transform your space into a haven of healing and unity, fostering deeper connection.

Why clearing emotional energy matters

Emotional energy is like the air you breathe—invisible but ever-present, shaping your home's atmosphere. Walk into a room filled with laughter, and you feel warmth. Step into one where an argument has lingered, and the tension clings on, even if the words have faded. Over time, these energetic imprints can build up. In blended families, this energy is layered with complexity. Each member brings emotional baggage—divorce, loss, or the challenge of blending traditions—that settles into shared spaces like a fog, subtly influencing moods and interactions.

For children in blended families, this energy can feel especially heavy. Kids are sensitive to vibrational shifts, picking up on unspoken tension from co-parenting conflicts or past homes. A stepchild might feel like an outsider in a living room carrying the residue of a parent's frustration. Emotional energy hits blended families hard. Parents, too, may unknowingly carry guilt or stress, affecting the home's chi. Over time, these imprints create a disconnected ecosystem, draining harmony and amplifying small conflicts.

A powerful way to clear these invisible barriers is by recognizing and releasing stuck energy, not just within our hearts but also within our living spaces. Clearing energy helps a blended family step into a new season. When you take the time to clear emotional energy, you create a blank slate, a space where everyone can start afresh. Families that engage in regular energy-clearing rituals tend to recover more quickly from conflicts. Clear this energy by involving kids in simple ceremonies, like ringing a bell together to signal a fresh start. For example, let a stepchild choose a chime sound, giving them a sense of ownership in the home's new energy. This small act says, "*You belong here*," fostering unity.

Cleansing the energy is akin to cracking a car window to clear away any fog and condensation with fresh air. It reduces emotional triggers and builds resilience, making your home a brave space for processing emotions. It's a reset, signaling that everyone has a place in this new chapter.

A worldwide look back

For centuries, cultures have recognized that a home's energy shapes its inhabitants' well-being and used rituals to clear stagnation and invite renewal. These practices offer timeless wisdom for blended families seeking peace.

Indigenous cultures across the Americas have long practiced smudging to purify spaces. Burning sage or palo santo, they believed the smoke carried away negative spirits, resetting homes for healing and connection. Picture a Navajo elder waving sage smoke through a hogan (a traditional Navajo dwelling), the scent mingling with prayers for unity. This ritual mirrors how blended families can clear emotional residue to cultivate belonging.

In ancient China, Feng Shui masters cleared *sha chi*, or heavy energy, to restore balance. They struck gongs or bells, sending vibrations to break up negativity, and placed water features to symbolize vitality. Imagine a Chinese scholar ringing chimes and placing a fountain in a courtyard, its gentle trickle inviting calm. This approach guides blended families to harness the elements of sound and water to refresh their homes, creating space for harmony.

Across all these traditions, the underlying principle is the same: the energy of a space profoundly impacts the people who inhabit it. These ancient practices remind blended families that clearing energy is a universal tool for connection and a way to nurture the emotional and spiritual health of everyone who enters.

The energy behind emotional clearing

During my first space clearing in a blended family home, I felt like I was stepping into a house that had been sealed shut for years. My Feng Shui mentor emphasized the importance of grounding and protecting oneself during the process, but I didn't fully understand the significance of this advice until I felt it for myself. As I moved through the home, sage in one hand and chimes in the other, something very perplexing happened. My root chakra—the energy center tied to stability—suddenly pulsed, not with pain but with a fiery awareness. It was as if the home's heavy energy was speaking to me, revealing pockets of tension. In the living room, the chimes vibrated unevenly, struggling against resistance. The sage smoke hung thick, sluggish, signaling stuck energy. My teacher's words echoed in my mind: "*Stay curious. Your body will tell you what the space needs.*"

I realized the home was holding years of arguments and grief, its energy as dense as a winter storm. As I rang chimes and smudged, the atmosphere shifted. The chimes sang clearly, and the smoke began to rise smoothly. By the end, I was exhausted, as if I'd carried the home's emotional weight. I took a salt bath to reset my aura, reflecting on the power of this work. That day taught me that clearing energy isn't just a ritual—it's a way to give a home permission to breathe again.

After years of performing space clearings, this process has become second nature to me. Each home tells its own story, and if we listen closely, we can hear where love has flourished and where wounds have festered. What I've learned is that your body, your intuition, and your energy can speak to you in ways you may never have expected. You just have to be open to listening.

In blended families, emotional histories—resentment, transition, or loss—can linger in shared spaces, creating invisible barriers. Clearing this energy with rituals like smudging or bell ringing says, "*We are reclaiming this space.*" You're telling your family that the energy in your home is something you value and will protect. Cleansing energy doesn't erase those histories; rather, it creates a neutral, shared foundation where new connections can grow. It's empowering, like opening a window to let light flood in.

The science of emotional energy

Scientific findings align with what ancient practices have known for centuries—our environment affects our mental and emotional states. While energy clearing may not be common practice, science offers compelling explanations for why it works.

- **Fresh air clears minds.**[9] Research from the *Environmental Protection Agency* shows fresh air reduces stress levels and sharpens mental clarity. Open windows to refresh blended family homes, fostering calm and focus.

- **Sound soothes anxiety.**[10] A study in *Frontiers in Psychology* finds that vibrations from bells or chimes reduce anxiety by disrupting stagnant energy patterns. Sound cleansing creates harmony in stepfamily spaces.

- **Water features relax.**[11] A biophilic study from the *Journal of Environmental Psychology* reveals that water features, like indoor fountains, boost relaxation by mimicking natural rhythms. A small feature calms blended family tensions.

- **Smudging purifies spaces.**[12] A study from the *Journal of Ethnopharmacology* shows sage smudging reduces airborne bacteria by 94%, clearing energy. Smudging rituals invite peace in shared homes.

These facts show that clearing emotional energy shifts your home's atmosphere, strengthening family bonds. Let's dive into practical steps to make this happen.

How to clear emotional energy

Clearing emotional energy is simple yet transformative. Follow these intentional steps to create an energetic shift in your home:

1. **Open the space:** Start with a grounding meditation to set an intention before beginning the clearing process. Open windows and doors to invite fresh air in.

2. **Use sound:** Move clockwise around each room. Ring a bell, clap your hands, or use a singing bowl to shift the atmosphere. Vibrations break up stuck energy, refreshing the space.

3. **Introduce movement:** Rearrange furniture, shake out throw blankets, or even dance in the room. Physical movement stirs up stagnant energy, encouraging it to dissipate.

4. **Smudge:** Burn sage, palo santo, or incense, and let the smoke waft into corners, while visualizing negativity drifting away. Invite family members to join in, unifying the ritual.

5. **Visualize cleansing light:** In each room, imagine a soft golden light dissolving any lingering negativity and leaving the space feeling warm and inviting. Seal it in by speaking words of affirmation.

6. **Add water elements:** Place a small fountain or bowl of water mixed with essential oils in a shared area to symbolize renewal and flow. Check it weekly to keep the energy vibrant.

7. **Create a ritual:** Whether it's a weekly incense burning or a monthly decluttering session combined with sound cleansing, consistency keeps the energy of the home flowing.

In my own home, I practice a three-step space-clearing process (sound, smudging, and intention-setting) every Feng Shui New Year in February. As a blended family, we experience moments of sadness, arguments, and external energies from visitors, and this ritual ensures our space remains one of balance and renewal. It's amazing how much lighter and more connected our home feels after this deep, energetic cleanse.

Client Case Study

A friend called me, exhausted and desperate, seeking help to energetically cleanse her renovated 1960s home. Despite the recent remodel, their basement—the family hangout—had been ruined by a sewer backup and a major mold issue. But that wasn't all. She confessed that her 8-year-old stepson was seeing strange entities in the house. He described a creature with six legs and a long tail darting across the living room. On top of that, the husband admitted to hearing a man clearing his throat. She also experienced unsettling moments: shadows moving in her peripheral vision and the radio mysteriously switching from hits from the 2000s to 1970s tunes. The previous owners had experienced a death, likely in the house. "*I know this all sounds crazy,*" she said, "*but I feel like something is in this house, and I don't know what to do.*"

I've heard other stories just like hers, and I knew a space clearing would help. Using my three-step Feng Shui process—sound therapy with chimes, smudging with sage, and intention-setting—I cleared the stagnant energy. The basement pulsed with resistance, my root chakra pounding, but as I worked, the air lightened, like a long-held sigh being released. We set intentions for unity, involving the kids. My friend took photos of the same room before and after the clearing, and you could see the difference—rooms that looked dim and heavy before now appeared brighter, even though nothing had physically changed. As I left their home that day, I felt a deep sense of gratitude for being part of their journey to reclaim their space and their connection as a blended family.

Weeks later, she reported no more visions of creatures, shadows, or strange sounds. The basement became a joyful hangout, with fewer arguments and more laughter. "*It finally feels like this house is ours,*" she said. "*We're not sharing it with anyone—or anything—else.*" Months later, they told me it's now the go-to space for movie nights and deep conversations, the very connection they once thought was out of reach. This shift shows how clearing energy opens hearts, fostering connection in a home where energy needs lifting. That's the power of clearing emotional energy and moving away from the storm.

Did You Know?
- *Fresh air isn't just refreshing: it improves oxygen flow, boosting energy levels and mental clarity for everyone in the home.*

- *The sound of bells or chimes has been used in spiritual practices for centuries because of its ability to disrupt negative energy.*

- *Movement, such as dancing or rearranging furniture, has been shown to elevate mood and promote creativity.*

- *The scents from sage, incense, or essential oils activate areas of the brain associated with relaxation and emotional regulation.*

Your Turn

Clearing emotional energy can feel like a refreshing new start. Trust the process and let the energy of your home guide you toward connection and revitalization.

Mantra: "*When I release stagnant energy, I welcome peace and renewal.*" What you clear today makes space for tomorrow's possibilities.

1. **Assess your home's energy:** Which room feels heavy? Note any emotions or events tied to it.

2. **Reframe thoughts:** Picture the kind of interactions, love, and connection that you would like to manifest. How does reframing alter the mood of you and your home?

3. **Try a clearing ritual:** Smudge or ring a bell in one space. How does the room feel after?

4. **Involve the family:** Invite kids to join a clearing ritual (e.g., picking the time or where to start). What ritual feels right to implement with family? How does it shift their engagement? Then celebrate with a family walk.

Reflect and Record Your Progress: The day after cleansing, write down one or more positive changes in your home's energy or family interactions (e.g., "*The living room feels calmer, and we're spending more time together*"). How does the cleansed space feel different? How can clearing energy become a family ritual?

Clearing emotional energy isn't a one-time task; it's an ongoing practice that keeps your home feeling fresh, open, and full of possibility. You regularly clean your home of physical debris; now it's time to clean it of emotional debris. By repeatedly releasing what no longer serves your family, you're making space for the interactions of happiness you deserve.

Chapter 4

THE MORNING FLOW TO START THE DAY

HOW TO CREATE A MORNING ROUTINE THAT ENERGIZES YOUR FAMILY

"The way you start your day can determine the quality of your day."
—Robin Sharma

A morning routine is like the opening movement of a symphony, setting the tone, pace, and energy for what follows. The first notes aren't rushed—they're intentional, guiding the mood for the entire piece. In a blended family, a morning flow grounds each member, ensuring everyone feels seen and in sync, like instruments playing in harmony. However, when frustration builds, the energy of the entire day feels disjointed before it's even begun. When mornings start with calm and connection, the day unfolds with grace, like a melody that lifts the heart. The goal isn't to achieve a picture-perfect routine, but rather, to find your family's rhythm.

Will Smith and Jada Pinkett Smith found this rhythm in their blended family. With children from their own marriage and Will's son, Trey, from a previous marriage, their busy lives could easily spiral into chaos. Yet they prioritize purposeful mornings. Picture Jada setting out fresh fruit and protein, a nod to her West Indian grandmother's wisdom, as a coffee aroma fills the air. Will shares a joke, his contagious smile sparking giggles. The kids take turns sharing their day's plans, with Jada offering gentle encouragement. In interviews, Will describes these moments as vital for connection, ensuring each child feels supported. Jada emphasizes a peaceful atmosphere, grounding the family before their demanding schedules. Their mornings show that intentional routines create a vibrant, unified start. Your family can find this flow, transforming chaos into connection.

In this chapter, you'll learn how to craft a morning routine using Feng Shui to optimize your home's energy and how to apply life-coaching strategies to foster collaboration. And just like with a symphony, no two performances are ever the same. Some mornings will feel fluid and graceful; others may be full of off-key notes. But the more you practice, the easier it becomes to recover, to listen to each other's tempo, and to return to a shared rhythm. These tools will energize your blended family, creating a harmonious start to each day.

Why the morning flow matters

Mornings are the foundation of your day, shaping mood, energy, and interactions. These moments are more than just a time to get ready; they are a chance to align your family's intentions. In Feng Shui, mornings represent new beginnings, with fresh chi flowing through open spaces. A cluttered kitchen or chaotic entryway blocks this energy, while organized areas invite clarity and calm. A rushed start leaves kids frazzled at school and parents playing catch-up. However, a thoughtful morning routine aligns your family's rhythm, fostering peace and collaboration.

Blended families face unique morning challenges. Differing routines—one parent savoring a sit-down breakfast, another grabbing coffee on the go—can spark friction. Stepchildren may navigate varying expectations from different households, leading to stress. They may feel torn between routines, causing confusion that can spiral into additional negative emotions. Without intention, these differences create a disjointed start, like an orchestra without a conductor.

Mornings in blended families need flexibility and inclusion. A thoughtful morning routine can help mitigate the stress of transitions, improve communication, and set a tone of harmony for the day. Try creating shared rituals, like a quick gratitude circle, to unify the group. Let kids choose a breakfast playlist to feel involved, signaling, "*This is our morning.*" This fosters a sense of belonging and eases transitions.

For those who may already have an established routine or who think mornings are too hectic to improve, ask yourself, "*What could mornings feel like if they were intentional?*" Don't look at creating a flawless flow, but rather, a vibrational frequency that's more about progress and presence. Small shifts, like a shared affirmation or a tidy entryway, reduce stress and build connection. Picture a home where laughter replaces rushed complaints, and everyone leaves feeling grounded. Just like a symphony, the way your morning begins sets the emotional tone for the entire day.

A worldwide look back

Throughout history, mornings were seen as sacred times for renewal and preparation. Cultures have long used morning rituals to align energy and purpose, offering valuable lessons for blended families.

In ancient Rome, the morning ritual of *salutatio* went beyond its formal greeting and exhibited the cornerstone of social and familial order. Envision Roman citizens dressed in flowing togas, visiting patrons' homes, exchanging greetings amid the scent of fresh bread and incense. These morning visits weren't rushed; they were deliberate moments to reinforce bonds, setting a purposeful tone. For blended families, this historical ritual can inspire small but impactful morning check-ins that emphasize respect, patience, and alignment within the household.

In India, mornings are often steeped in rituals that blend spirituality and daily life. Many families begin the day by lighting a *diya* (oil lamp) in front of a home shrine, the flame symbolizing the removal of darkness and the arrival of light. Picture a family chanting together, their voices blending. Soft mantras and sandalwood incense create a grounding rhythm. This practice inspires blended families to share gratitude or intentions, creating a shared, harmonious start.

These historical examples remind us that mornings are more than just a rush to get out the door; they are opportunities to align with purpose and presence. In blended families, adopting elements from these traditions helps create shared rituals that reinforce understanding, lovingness, and positivity as you begin the day together.

The energy behind mornings

Mornings in my blended family are a symphony of contrasts. My oldest stepson, like my husband, leaps out of bed, buzzing with drive. The younger one hits snooze, needing gentle nudging—my role as the "backup alarm." Our daughter hovers between the two—not thrilled, but not resistant. I make it a point to set a positive tone for the household.

Despite our different approaches, we each carry our own energy into the morning. If mornings are stressful, that energy can ripple through the entire day. I focus on keeping things light, upbeat, and grounded. If time is against us, I play a game with my kids to determine who can finish what task faster. "*Let's see who can put on their socks the fastest,*" or "*Who's going to win the race to the car?*" The kids thrive on wanting to beat Mom, and I succeed in getting everyone to move faster—a win-win! These small moments of fun transform hurried mornings into something enjoyable.

Whether we're sleepy, energized, or somewhere in between, there's always room for a shared moment of gratitude; perhaps it's appreciation for the beautiful sunrise or simply the gift of a new day. One of my favorite morning rituals is meditating as soon as I wake up. This simple practice helps me stay calm, even when mornings inevitably become taxing amongst our blended family. My heart chakra, tied to love and connection, used to tighten when mornings turned chaotic, with rushed breakfasts and misplaced shoes. Reflecting on my years before I began doing morning mindfulness practices, I discerned a very noticeable difference in my stress and cortisol levels.

The important thing is to recognize that every family member may have their own preferences and routines. Mornings don't have to be a battle of wills; instead, they can be like a puzzle, where each piece fits together to create a harmonious flow. Contemplate what works and what doesn't, and be open to tweaking the routine as needed. Pay attention to how the energy feels in your home, both among the people and within the space itself. By staying flexible and focusing on positive, higher-vibration energy, you can discover how mornings can be a source of connection, like music to the ears.

The science of mornings

The way in which we begin our day influences cognitive function, resilience, and stress levels, making mornings crucial for establishing positive habits. Research shows that morning routines impact emotional and mental well-being.

- **Routines boost focus.**[13] Studies from the *National Sleep Foundation* find that morning routines allow the brain to transition smoothly from rest to alertness, improving focus, cognitive performance, and decision-making. Planned-out mornings strengthen blended family clarity.

- **Rituals reduce stress.**[14] A study from *Psychological Science* shows that families with structured morning routines experience lower stress levels and more harmonious interactions throughout the day. Consistent rituals unite stepfamilies in calm connections.

- **Rituals facilitate bonds.**[15] Research from *Emotion*, demonstrates that families who engage in shared morning rituals report stronger emotional bonds and improved mood regulation. A ritual like family breakfasts nurtures stepchild trust.

- **Clear spaces = clear minds.**[16] A study from the *Journal of Environmental Psychology* states that cluttered or disorganized spaces create mental overload, making it harder to stay calm and focused. A pleasant morning environment promotes clarity and emotional balance, supporting blended family stability.

These findings confirm that a morning flow improves efficiency and nurtures a peaceful, connected household. Let's explore specific ways to create a morning routine that works for your blended family.

How to create a morning flow

Blending Feng Shui's environmental harmony with the intentional habits drawn from life coaching' creates an optimal morning flow. These steps will energize your family:

1. **Set the tone the night before:** Preparation is key to a smooth morning. Pack lunches, lay out clothes, and organize backpacks before bedtime. Tidy the entryway to ensure smooth chi flow. A little effort in the evening prevents morning chaos.

2. **Incorporate gratitude:** Begin the day by sharing one thing each person is thankful for, supporting positivity. A bowl of stones on the table can hold words of appreciation, symbolizing unity. Gratitude reshapes neural pathways, improving emotional well-being and resilience.

3. **Create personal moments:** Allow five minutes for individual rituals. Whether it's a quiet reflection, stretching, journaling, or meditation, this time can help everyone feel grounded and respected before coming together.

4. **Gather together:** Establish a central spot, like the kitchen table, where everyone gathers for a few moments each morning. Use this time to connect, share the day's plans, or simply enjoy breakfast together.

5. **Simplify breakfast:** Choose easy, healthy options like smoothies, fresh fruit, or preprogrammed coffee with MCT oil. Simplifying breakfast ensures everyone starts the day nourished without added stress.

6. **Use visual cues:** Create a family checklist or morning schedule and post it where everyone can see. Visual reminders keep the routine clear and reduce the need for repeated instructions.

7. **End with encouragement:** Before heading out the door, share a quick word of encouragement or family affirmation. A simple "*You've got this*" or "*Let's make it a great day*" can set a positive tone.

Begin formulating what change you could make tonight to set a smoother tone for tomorrow morning. These steps tune your blended family's morning symphony to create a vibrant start.

Client Case Study

One blended family that I coached faced chaotic mornings. With five kids from two marriages, arguments persisted over bathroom time, missing items, and even who was getting what for lunch. The parents described mornings as their most stressful time of day, setting a tense tone for everyone.

We identified pain points—unspoken expectations and no structure—and created a "command center." A gratitude ritual was also added, where everyone shared something that they looked forward to that day. Initially, the kids resisted, but the visual cues and appreciation empowered them.

The family command center became the go-to spot for organization and communication and comprised of four main parts: 1) a family calendar to track school events, extracurricular activities, and appointments; 2) a bulletin board for important reminders and permission slips; 3) hooks and cubbies, which were labeled with each child's name for backpacks, shoes, and lunch bags; and 4) a chore chart, to divide morning responsibilities clearly and fairly. These duties were balanced between the kids who were there full time and those who were there part time.

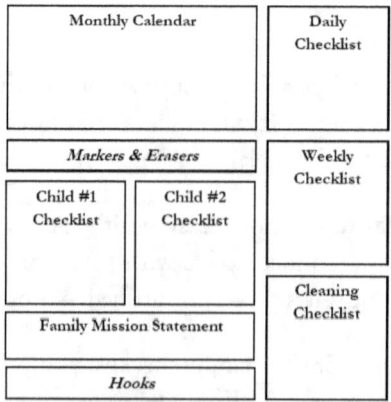

A family command center layout.

The command center created a go-to instruction spot and eliminated the need for constant reminders. It also inspired the kids to take ownership of their tasks, reducing last-minute scrambles. The sense of order brought immediate relief and clarity.

After a few weeks, the family noticed a transformation. The checklist reduced the number of arguments, and the gratitude ritual brought a sense of calm and connection to their mornings. One of the teens even started making breakfast for the younger kids as part of his contribution, which strengthened sibling relationships. The command center became a hub of efficiency, ensuring everyone knew their responsibilities and could work together seamlessly.

Before we worked together, their mornings had felt like a noisy musical warm-up with everyone out of sync. Through a few intentional changes, like setting expectations the night before and creating visual cues, they found their rhythm. Now, mornings feel like a well-rehearsed ensemble: still human, still imperfect, but unmistakably in tune. The parents reported that mornings had gone from being a dreaded chore to a time they genuinely enjoyed as a family. Six months later, they still use the command center and told me it had helped reduce tardiness, forgotten items, and morning arguments dramatically. It was order that everyone hadn't even realized that they needed.

Did You Know?

- *Families who eat breakfast together at least three times a week report stronger relationships and better communication.*

- *Starting the day with physical activity, like a short family walk, can boost mood and energy levels for everyone.*

- *Listening to calming music or nature sounds in the morning can reduce stress and create a peaceful environment.*

- *Spending even five minutes outside in natural light can improve your mood and set the body's internal clock for better focus and sleep later.*

Your Turn

When approached with intention, the morning flow serves as a foundation for deeper family connection, reduced stress, and a happier home environment. Craft a morning flow to energize your family by starting with one step and observing the shift.

Mantra: "*When we start with intention, we set the tone for the day.*" Begin with mindfulness and watch how mornings shape momentum and interactions.

1. **Identify morning stressors:** What moments in your family's morning feel chaotic or rushed? Why?

2. **Try a ritual:** Introduce a small, meaningful practice like a gratitude circle, a shared breakfast, or a calming playlist. What rituals are for individuals? Which are for the family?

3. **Involve family:** Invite everyone to contribute ideas for making mornings more enjoyable. How does this shift dynamics? What kind of check-ins work best for your partner or the kids?

4. **Be consistent:** Stick with your morning flow for at least two to three weeks. Rituals take time to become habits, so allow space for adjustments. Will you be the one following up, or will this be a shared effort? What will be the motivation to continue?

Reflect and Record Your Progress: After you've established a new family morning routine, write down one or more positive changes in your home's energy or family interactions (e.g., "*The kitchen feels so organized, and the kids are empowered to contribute*"). Has the new morning ritual created a sense of calm and connection? How can a morning flow become a family tradition?

Mornings are your family's opportunity to align with intention and positivity, setting the stage for a fabulous day ahead. Consider how small adjustments started a ripple effect for the rest of your day and your relationships. These steps create a home where connections become a beautifully orchestrated symphony.

Chapter 5

THE FAMILY ROOM RESET

HOW THE FAMILY ROOM CULTIVATES COMFORT AND JOYFUL INTERACTIONS

"A room should never allow the eye to settle in one place. It should smile at you and create fantasy."
—Juan Montoya

The family room is like a campfire, drawing everyone to its warmth. Its glow invites stories, laughter, and quiet moments, knitting hearts together despite the chill of daily life. In a blended family, this space is vital—a neutral ground where stepchildren, parents, and siblings can shed tensions and connect, their voices mingling like crackling logs. A well-tended fire, arranged with care, burns brightly; a neglected one sputters, leaving a cold lifelessness. Resetting your family room with intention creates a haven for joy and unity and for the fire to burn even brighter.

Reese Witherspoon and Ryan Phillippe understand the importance of creating a campfire-like spark in their blended family. Even after their divorce, Reese and Ryan prioritized building stability and connection in co-parenting their children, ensuring that both homes felt equally warm and familiar. Reese speaks on how intentional décor—like a cozy family room filled with inviting textures, sentimental décor, and conversational areas—helps maintain a sense of home no matter where their children are located. In her book *Whiskey in a Teacup: What Growing Up in the South Taught Me About Life, Love, and Baking Biscuits* (Touchstone, 2018), Witherspoon highlights the significance of ambience: *"It's important to me that my home feel welcoming. I want people to feel like they can sit on the furniture. You can have a beautiful house, very well décorated, but you have to be able to sit down or else it's not a home."* Her family room includes aspects of relaxation, but more importantly, a deliberate space to gather and connect. This aligns with Feng Shui's emphasis on fostering positive energy through accessible, livable environments. Reese and her family understand that while life may be busy, the time spent together is what strengthens the foundation of a blended family. Your family can create this warmth, too.

In this chapter, you'll learn to reset your family room using Feng Shui to enhance comfort and energy flow, paired with life coaching strategies to encourage joyful interactions. These tools will transform your blended family's gathering space into a sanctuary of togetherness, where memories are made and bonds deepen, setting a harmonious ambience.

Why the family room matters

The family room is your home's emotional core, where shared moments shape relationships. Its energy influences how family members interact—whether they feel safe to open up, or guarded amid clutter and chaos. In Feng Shui, this room is one of the most important spaces because it represents connection, harmony, and a shared energy among loved ones. Good Feng Shui radiates throughout the entire home, its chi flowing freely, which enhances success in other areas of life. A poorly designed family room stifles joy, leaving interactions strained or distant.

Blended families often struggle with family room dynamics. Stepchildren may feel like outsiders if the room reflects one parent's history over another's, with photos or furniture from past homes dominating. Cluttered corners or cramped seating can amplify tension, making gatherings feel forced. Differing preferences—teens craving tech, younger kids wanting play space—can spark conflicts, leaving the room divisive. Or parents who may be underusing the room because it's become a dumping ground for toys, laundry, or forgotten items, leading to feelings of stress or frustration.

A family room reset offers a solution. By creating an inclusive, comfortable space, you signal that everyone belongs. It creates an environment where conversations flow easily, and where laughter and relaxation occur naturally. Involving stepchildren in choosing décor fosters ownership, easing transitions between households. A Feng Shui-inspired layout, with open pathways and soft lighting, encourages warmth and connection. This reset transforms the room into a hub where blended families build shared memories, from movie nights to heart-to-heart talks.

By intentionally designing this room, keeping all family members in mind, it cultivates an atmosphere that supports your family's emotional welfare. Like a campfire drawing in weary travelers, a reset family room invites bonding. It reduces friction and nurtures joy, making every gathering a step toward unity.

A worldwide look back

For centuries, cultures have crafted communal spaces to foster connection, offering wisdom for blended families for resetting their family rooms. These spaces were designed to balance individual needs with collective unity, much like today's family rooms.

In ancient Greece, the *andron* was a communal room where families gathered for meals and storytelling. Picture a stone hearth flickering, clay cups clinking, and voices echoing with tales. Furniture was arranged in circles to encourage equality, ensuring chi-like energy flowed freely. These spaces weren't just practical: they were designed to advance community and connection, making everyone feel valued and included. This setup inspires blended families to arrange seating inclusively to promote open dialogue.

In medieval Europe, the *hearth* was the heart of the home. Families huddled around its warmth, sharing stories amid the scent of burning wood. Parents and elders gathered to impart advice, make decisions, and connect with children. The open layout ensured everyone had a place, fostering a coalition despite diverse roles. This practice encourages blended families to create flexible, welcoming family rooms that invite everyone to bond.

For blended families, these historical examples offer valuable lessons. A well-designed gathering space—whether it's an *andron*, a *hearth*, or a family room—isn't just about functionality. It's about creating a space where every family member feels represented, included, and valued.

The energy behind family rooms

Our first starter home came with a loft that we used as our family room. We had this big L-shaped couch that all four of us would snuggle up on. The boys were younger then—still small enough to curl up under the mounds of blankets and pillows, while we watched our regular family TV shows. The lighting was tranquil, the layout comfortable, as if we were sitting around a warm campfire.

Life evolved, and so did our needs. When our daughter was born, we quickly outgrew that home. In our new house, we reluctantly moved the beloved L-shaped couch to the basement because the family room layout couldn't accommodate it. We replaced it with mismatched furniture from my old apartment. The size was off, the style was off, and the layout just didn't feel right. We stopped spending as much time together. The closeness and connection we'd built in our cozy loft felt like it was fading.

At first, we chalked it up to life changes, the boys spending more time with friends, the demands of caring for a baby, and the busyness of everyday routines. I desperately wanted our family room to be a space where we could connect again. So, I took intentional Feng Shui-inspired steps and transformed the space by:

- **Following the Goldilocks rule:** I purchased new furniture that fit the space—not too big, not too small, but just right. This allowed the room to feel proportionate and balanced, ensuring energy wasn't blocked and creating a sense of flow.

- **Creating a cozy ambience:** I hung drapes and softened the lighting with table lamps and dimmable bulbs. This added warmth and intimacy to the room, encouraging relaxation and togetherness.

- **Grounding the space:** I made sure that each couch and chair was anchored with a side table or sofa table. This grounding technique stabilized the energy in the room, making it feel secure and welcoming.

- **Establishing visual connection:** I hung family photos that included our entire blended family, and committed to updating them regularly. Seeing these memories created a sense of belonging and reminded us of our shared journey as a family.

- **Maintaining peace with organization:** I added a designated toy box that matched the décor, keeping the space neat and tidy while still functional for our daughter's playtime.

The shift was electric. It transformed our family room into one of the most loved spaces in our new home. Now, we spend evenings and weekends together, watching shows, sharing stories, and soaking in the uplifting energy we've created. My favorite part? The sound of laughter and sense of bonding as a family of five. For blended families, a deliberately planned family room becomes a neutral ground, a symbol of unity, and a reflection of the love and connection you want to foster.

The science of the family room reset

Research shows that the design of a family room impacts emotional and social well-being. Its layout and energy shape how families connect, making a reset essential for harmony.

- **Spatial psychology matters.**[17] A study from the *Journal of Environ-*

mental Psychology states that circular seating and open designs reduce stress, sparking interaction. Blended families thrive in spaces that promote connection.

- **Shared activities build bonds.**[18] The *National Council on Family Relations* highlights that families who regularly engage in shared activities experience stronger emotional bonds and higher overall satisfaction in their relationships. Shared rituals boost stepfamily harmony and joy.

- **Warm colors lift moods.**[19] A study from the *Color Research and Application* journal affirms that warm tones, like earthy greens, boost mood and comfort. Cozy hues create inviting spaces for blended families.

- **Personal touches enhance belonging.**[20] Studies from *Applied Environmental Psychology* demonstrate that incorporating personal elements enhances a sense of belonging. Customized spaces unite stepfamilies emotionally.

These findings confirm that a reset family room fosters joy and unity. With a few practical steps, you too can create a warm and magnetic environment in your own home.

How to reset your family room

Resetting your family room blends Feng Shui's spatial harmony with life coaching's collaborative spirit. These steps create a joyful hub that transforms it into the heart of your household.

1. **Declutter:** Clear excess furniture and outdated items. Keep only what sparks joy or serves a purpose, encouraging the chi to flow.

2. **Create zones for different activities:** Designate areas for family activities, such as a reading nook, a game corner, or a spot for puzzles. This ensures the room meets everyone's needs.

3. **Rearrange furniture:** Next, arrange seating in a way that encourages face-to-face interaction and establishes designated zones. Ensure clear pathways for the movement of energy.

4. **Add a gathering element:** Consider adding a centralized element like a coffee table or ottoman that invites interaction and acts as a place to gather communal snacks or board games.

5. **Incorporate comfortable textures:** Once bigger furniture is placed, focus on the smaller items. Add soft throw blankets, plush pillows, and fluffy rugs to create a sense of warmth and comfort. Think of this space as a cozy campfire.

6. **Use neutral colors:** Opt for a color palette that feels inviting and peaceful, such as soft grays, blues, creams, and earth tones. These colors promote relaxation and harmony.

7. **Display meaningful décor:** Include photos, art, or objects that reflect your family's identity. Let each family member choose a décor item to foster ownership and inclusion.

8. **Consider your lighting:** End with the overall ambience. Layer your lighting with options for different moods. Use dimmable overhead lights, table lamps, and even candles to create a tranquil atmosphere.

Once your family room has been reset, you'll notice how small changes create a ripple effect on your family's connection and energy. What makes these changes impactful isn't just the design; it's the intention behind them.

Client Case Study

One of the most impactful stories I learned during my Feng Shui training was about a family struggling with disconnection and cohesion. The parents reached out to our Feng Shui teacher because their teenage son was severely depressed and expressed feelings of isolation. His parents noticed that he would retreat to his bedroom rather than spending time in the family room with the rest of the household. He confided that he often felt like he didn't belong in the family because he was a "stepson" and even questioned his own existence. Naturally, the parents were heartbroken, worried, and at a loss after trying everything.

When our teacher arrived at their home, she immediately noticed an issue as she walked through the front door. In Feng Shui, the entrance is another important area because it is the primary gateway where the "mouth of chi" enters and flows into your living spaces. On the foyer console table was a large family vacation photo. It was a lovely picture... except the son wasn't in it. He had missed the trip, and while the omission seemed small, it spoke volumes about how he felt excluded. As our teacher went to the family room, she realized that nearly every framed family photo in the room featured past vacations or moments from before their family had blended, and he was missing, except for one. Without realizing it, the space itself was reinforcing his sense of exclusion.

During the Feng Shui consultation, she suggested replacing the entrance photo and the family room photos. The parents took her advice, swapping them with all family members and even adding ones of just the son. They also made sure he had a say in which pictures were displayed, allowing him to feel included in shaping the space. As they did, they described an immediate emotional shift: a sense of wholeness they hadn't realized was missing. The son saw himself represented, and for the first time in months, he smiled when he walked through the door.

Within weeks, mealtime conversations grew livelier, and the household felt lighter and more connected. The energy in the space shifted—it was no longer just a reflection of the past but a representation of the new family they were building together. The teen son who once retreated now spends time with the family playing games, watching shows, and even suggesting movie nights—something the parents had given up hope on. This transformation reinforced an important truth: the design of a space can either strengthen family bonds or deepen divisions, even without conscious awareness. With a few intentional changes, they were able to create a family room that invited connection, belonging, and warmth for everyone.

Did You Know?
- *Families who spend at least four evenings a week in a shared space report stronger relationships and better communication.*

- *Adding greenery, such as potted plants, can improve air quality and create a sense of calm.*

- *Soft lighting, like lamps or string lights, promotes relaxation and can make family rooms feel more inviting.*

- *Incorporating scents like lavender or vanilla enhances the atmosphere and reduces stress levels.*

Your Turn

Every family's needs are unique, so consider what changes will bring the most joy, comfort, and harmony. Start with small steps and let intention guide you toward a space where your blended family thrives.

Mantra: "*When we shape our surroundings, we shape our connections.*" Every design choice is an opportunity to create warmth, closeness, and belonging.

1. **Assess the family room:** Take note of what feels inviting and what doesn't. What feels "off" in your family room? Clutter, layout, or energy? Why? Are there any underutilized areas?

2. **Feel into the space:** Close your eyes and visualize. What energy do you want this space to have? Should it feel calming, energizing, or playful?

3. **Prioritize function:** How do you want to use the family room? Are there any activities—like movie nights, board games, or quiet reading time—that you'd like to encourage?

4. **Focus on family:** Is everyone represented in the room? Are there elements—like photos, décor, or shared items—that reflect each family member's identity and make each individual feel included?

Reflect and Record Your Progress: After one week of resetting, write down one or more positive changes in your family room's energy or interactions (e.g., "*The room feels open, and we're playing games together*"). How does the space feel different? What new memories are forming? How can this reset become a family tradition?

Your family room is your home's campfire—a place for warmth and stories. Every step creates a space where joy flourishes and the embers continue to burn brightly.

Chapter 6

THE BEDROOM AS A SANCTUARY

HOW TO RESTORE LOVE, PEACE, AND RESTFULNESS FOR PARENTS AND KIDS

"A good laugh and a long sleep are the best cures in the doctor's book."
—Irish proverb

The bedroom is a quiet harbor, sheltering your spirit from life's stormy seas. After navigating school runs, work demands, and family tensions, it offers a calm bay where soft lighting and plush textures invite you to exhale. In a blended family, where dynamics can feel choppy, this sacred space becomes vital. Whether it's a child's bedroom offering stability between households or the shared bedroom between partners who need unity amidst co-parenting complexities, these serve as anchor points, both emotionally and energetically. Just as a harbor protects vessels from stormy seas, your bedroom should protect your energy. When you enter your bedroom, it should feel like gently docking a ship in a peaceful bay, where relationships are renewed, dreams take flight, and deep rest restores both body and heart.

The British Royal Family—a blended dynasty—cherishes bedroom sanctuaries. When Prince Charles and Princess Diana divorced, and later when Charles married Camilla, their family dynamic shifted significantly. Reports from insiders emphasized how important it was for their private spaces, particularly their bedrooms, to reflect harmony, fluidity, and individuality for the new family unit. In fact, efforts were made to create welcoming, neutral spaces where family members could feel at ease amidst public scrutiny. It became a place where distinct journeys quietly converged, anchoring diverse histories and dreams into a shared reserve of comfort and peace. These intimate spaces have become havens for rest and healing, highlighting how these bedrooms play a critical role in maintaining balance and rest after a day in the public eye. Their approach shows that intentionally designed bedrooms strengthen blended families, even complex ones. Your family can create this peace, too.

In this chapter, you'll learn to build bedroom sanctuaries using Feng Shui to optimize energy flow, and life coaching techniques to nurture emotional safety. These tools will transform your blended family's bedrooms into harbors of love, peace, and rest, bolstering connections and well-being.

Why the bedroom matters

Bedrooms are your home's private ports, where rest and renewal shape health and relationships. Their energy impacts sleep, intimacy, and security, crucial for blended families navigating complex undercurrents. In Feng Shui, the bedroom is another vital space in your home because it directly influences your physical and emotional welfare. Since we spend nearly one-third of our lives sleeping, optimal energy in this space is crucial to keep the chi flowing. A well-balanced bedroom fosters deep relaxation, love, and rejuvenation, essential for an anchored life. A chaotic bedroom disrupts the flow of chi, which strains bonds and well-being.

Blended families face unique bedroom challenges. Parents' bedrooms, when cluttered with ex-partners' items or mismatched styles, can stifle intimacy, weakening the family's core. Stepchildren, shuttling between homes, may feel insecure if their rooms lack personal touches or carry past families' relics, which may produce apprehension and self-doubt. Kids' differing needs—teens craving privacy, younger ones fearing shadows—can make shared spaces tense, amplifying feelings of displacement.

A bedroom sanctuary offers a solution. Personalized, soothing rooms signal belonging, anchoring stepchildren across households. For parents, a serene bedroom nurtures love and partnership, ensuring they have the emotional bandwidth to lead their family with love and patience. A bedroom that is thoughtfully designed to reflect a child's personality and provides consistency can make all the difference in their relaxation and confidence. Involving kids in décor choices builds ownership, eases transitions, and fosters trust. Feng Shui elements, like calming colors and clear spaces, promote restful sleep and emotional safety. Like a harbor sheltering ships, a bedroom sanctuary restores balance. It reduces anxiety and deepens connection, creating a room where love and rest thrive.

A worldwide look back

Cultures have long designed bedrooms as sacred havens, balancing rest and emotional well-being, offering wisdom for blended families. These spaces were crafted to promote peace, much like today's bedrooms.

In ancient China, Feng Shui principles shaped bedrooms for harmony. Beds were placed in the *command position*, facing the door but not aligned, ensuring a sense of safety and optimal chi flow. The placement was about creating an energetic balance, making the room feel secure and restful. Picture a silk canopy framing a bed, incense wafting, as sleepers could see the door but weren't directly in line with it to feel protected. This inspires blended families to position beds thoughtfully, promoting stability for kids and adults.

In medieval Europe, bedrooms often doubled as places of intimate refuge. Heavy curtains surrounded bedposts to provide both heat and privacy, fashioning an intimate, cocoon-like environment. The soft flicker of candlelight added a soothing ambience to the room. Imagine families sinking into plush linens, the scent of beeswax calming them to reconnect with themselves or loved ones. Blended families can mirror this practice by using soft textures and warm lighting to create security and unity.

These historical practices remind us that the bedroom has primary and secondary functions. For blended families, drawing inspiration from these traditions can help create bedrooms that support love, peace, and connection, along with sleep.

The energy behind bedrooms

Growing up, my bedroom was my quiet harbor. I had a queen bed anchored by shelves with soft pastel wallpaper depicting forest animals frolicking over rolling hills. It was comforting as I felt grounded and could easily drift off to sleep. The space was sweet, safe, and suited to my childhood self, especially for someone who loves connecting to nature, even at an early age.

Then one day, my mom decided it was time for a change. She wanted my room to reflect my growing maturity. The queen bed was replaced by a metal-framed daybed with vertical bars and a matching trundle underneath. The new bed sat under the window with a mirrored vanity directly across from where I slept. At first, it seemed like just another design upgrade, but soon, my sleep became unsettled. I didn't feel the same sense of peace and security as before. My newfound restlessness was chalked up to puberty, hormones, and teenage angst, but now, as a Feng Shui expert, I see things differently.

Here's what I recommend for a great night's sleep—and why my sleep changed:

- **Have nothing stored under the bed.** In Feng Shui, it's highly recommended that the space under the bed remains clear, allowing energy to flow freely. Having a metal-framed trundle underneath blocks the chi. Additionally, the metal element is known to bring flightiness that disrupts the intended grounding energy for sleep.

- **Have no metal slat frames.** Solid fabric headboards or wooden bed frames provide supporting energy, promoting deeper sleep and relaxation. Metal slat bed frames subconsciously resemble prison bars, making the sleeper feel trapped or unsettled.

- **Have no beds below windows.** When a bed is directly beneath a window, the energy around the sleeper is less protected. In Feng Shui, windows symbolize movement and transitions, and placing a bed in this position can cause restlessness, as the spirit may feel as if it's drifting outward rather than staying close to the body.

- **Have no mirrors facing the bed.** Mirrors have reflective properties that can disrupt sleep by bouncing energy around the room. They can also create confusion for the spirit, making rest less restorative. If positioned directly across from the bed, they can cause unease in the subconscious, even if you don't consciously notice them.

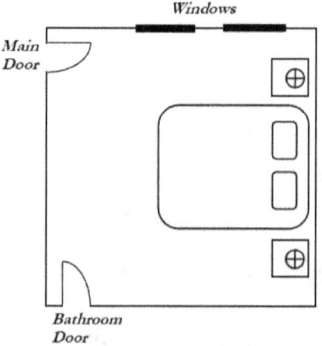

An example of the bedroom command position.

Looking back, I know my mom had the best intentions; she wanted my room to grow with me, and I loved her for doing her best to achieve that. Now that I understand Feng Shui, I've used this knowledge to ensure all bedrooms in our home are designed for the most restful and supportive energy possible. As a blended family, I want each person to feel like their room is a place of peace, belonging, and cozy comfort.

By incorporating these Feng Shui principles, you too can create a bedroom that feels like a true sanctuary—one that promotes deep sleep, emotional well-being, and intimate relationships.

The science of restful spaces

Research shows that bedroom design affects sleep, mood, and relationships. A sanctuary-like space promotes rest and connection, vital for blended families.

- **Clean bedrooms boost sleep.**[21] Research from the *National Sleep Foundation* finds that a clean, comfortable, and calming bedroom improves sleep duration and quality. Restful spaces nurture blended family well-being.

- **Clutter-free rooms ease stress.**[22] A study from the *Health Psychology* journal states that clutter-free bedrooms reduce anxiety, lower cortisol levels, and help the nervous system relax to boost rest. Serene sanctuaries calm stepfamily tensions.

- **Personalized spaces deepen bonds.**[23] Research from the *Journal of Environmental Psychology* discusses how personalized spaces enhance emotional security, which can improve intimacy and communication. A relaxing and inviting atmosphere creates intimacy in blended homes.

- **Calming colors and lighting aid sleep.** Studies from *Sleep Medicine* show that calming colors improve sleep quality,[24] while *Neuroscience Letters* finds harsh lighting spikes anxiety, disrupting rest.[25] Add creams, light blues, and soft lighting to free a blended home of stress and discomfort.

These findings highlight that a harbor-like bedroom fosters peace and unity, when designed with intention. Let's explore practical steps to create this space.

How to create a sanctuary bedroom

Creating a bedroom sanctuary blends Feng Shui's calming energy with life coaching's emotional focus. These steps foster love and rest:

1. **Declutter for peace:** Begin by removing items that don't belong in the bedroom. When you have items like a computer or treadmill, these signal to your brain it's time to be active, not rest.

2. **Create relaxation zones:** Designate spaces for specific activities, such as a cozy reading nook or a spot for journaling. This ensures the room feels functional yet restful. Zones should be limited to relaxation-type activities.

3. **Position the bed thoughtfully:** Place the bed in the *command position*, where it has a clear view of the door but isn't directly in line with it. This arrangement promotes a sense of security and relaxation versus the coffin position—when aligned directly with the entrance.

4. **Choose calming colors:** Paint walls in a soothing color palette, such as light blues, greens, or neutrals. These colors promote relaxation and improve sleep quality.

5. **Add soft textures:** Next, focus on smaller bedroom décor. Use plush bedding and curtains to create warmth. A cozy throw invites relaxation. Choose soft, breathable fabrics and layers that invite you to unwind.

6. **Incorporate personal touches:** In children's bedrooms, let kids choose the décor (e.g., posters, stuffed animals). Parents can add meaningful items that celebrate the relationship. Feng Shui states that there should be no photos of children in the parents' bedroom.

7. **Focus on lighting:** End with a restful ambience. Use warm, dimmable lighting to create a calming atmosphere. Avoid harsh overhead lights and consider adding bedside lamps or fairy lights for a softer glow.

These steps build a harbor of peace that nurtures your family's well-being. By taking the time to create a bedroom that feels like a sanctuary, you're both improving sleep and ensuring that everyone in your blended family has a space that feels like home.

Client Case Study

One of my clients had a little boy who was terrified of sleeping in his own room. Every night, he would tell his parents about the "shadow man" that appeared in the corner, whispering that he felt watched and unsafe. His sleep was restless, and he often ended up sneaking into his parents' bed or sleeping in the hallway outside their door. His parents, exhausted and concerned, reached out to me for help.

As I assessed his room, I noticed some Feng Shui red flags. From the bed's positioning and the beam overhead, to the clutter and electronics, all contributed to a chaotic energy that was disrupting his sleep.

The first step in restoring peace involved performing a space clearing. I used chimes and sage to cleanse the energy, setting the intention of calmness, protection, and release from those lingering shadows. Then, we addressed the layout of the room by:

- **Moving the bed away from the wall** to allow energy to flow freely around it. This subtle shift created a sense of openness and security.

- **Softening the beam's heaviness** by adding a soft fabric canopy around it, which visually lifted the immensity and pressure, creating an angelic feeling of protection.

- **Clearing out clutter** to make space for calm, harmonious energy. We introduced storage bins that matched the décor to maintain tidiness without feeling sterile.

- **Minimizing electronics near the bed** and replacing them with a salt lamp. The soft amber glow neutralized excess electromagnetic energy.

Within a few days, his parents reported that their son's sleep had improved dramatically. He no longer talked about the "shadow man," and bedtime became a peaceful, welcome routine instead of a nightly battle. The child even started to keep his room tidy and inviting, without being told to do so. His newfound sense of security in his space transformed not only his sleep but also his overall mood and confidence. Even his teachers noted improved focus and fewer emotional outbursts at school, which his parents directly attributed to the new calm in his environment. The parents were no longer worried and were able to get sleep for themselves as well.

For blended families, this case highlights how a bedroom is more than just a place to sleep; it provides emotional grounding. Ensuring children's rooms feel safe and welcoming can make all the difference in how they transition to a new family dynamic.

Did You Know?

- *Using blackout curtains can improve sleep by blocking out light and creating a darker, more restful environment.*

- *Incorporating lavender or chamomile scents in your bedroom can promote relaxation and reduce anxiety.*

- *Keeping electronic devices out of the bedroom or on airplane mode improves sleep quality by minimizing distractions and blue light exposure.*

- *Weighted blankets have been shown to reduce nervousness and improve sleep for both adults and children.*

Your Turn

By designing a bedroom haven, you develop stronger bonds and deeper connections. Small intentional changes can lead to profound transformations in comfort, peace, and protection.

Mantra: *"When I create a sanctuary, I nurture love and rest."* Rest is not a luxury—it's essential, so allow the home to support this deep and meaningful relaxation.

1. **Assess each bedroom:** Walk through the bedrooms and take note of what feels inviting and what doesn't. What may be disrupting sleep? Clutter, colors, or layout? Why?

2. **Declutter and refresh:** Are there any unnecessary items that can be removed to refresh the space? What changes—like lighting, bed positioning, or personal touches—can you make today to create a more peaceful environment?

3. **Involve your family:** Encourage family members to participate in designing their bedrooms. Ask what feels meaningful and what doesn't. How does their input shift the family dynamics?

4. **Set a goal:** Stand at the bedroom door and picture your ideal vibe. What adjectives come to mind? What steps will get you there?

Reflect and Record Your Progress: After completing the action steps for one bedroom in your household, write down one or more positive changes in your bedroom's energy or family interactions (e.g., *"The kids' room feels calm, and they're sleeping better"*). How does the room feel different? What new sense of peace is forming?

Like any good harbor, a thoughtfully designed bedroom prepares you to launch again the next day, steadier, stronger, and more in tune with the tides of family life. Every step creates a space where tranquility expands, and nurturing love and rest settle.

Chapter 7

THE KITCHEN CONNECTION

HOW THE KITCHEN IMPACTS FAMILIES TO NOURISH MORE THAN BODIES

"The kitchen is where we come to understand our past and create our future."
—Marcus Samuelsson

The kitchen is the heart of the home, the vital organ that sustains, nourishes, and keeps the family alive. Like a heart pumping blood into every part of the body, the kitchen fuels the home with warmth, energy, and love. It pulses with movement—chopping, stirring, plating—just as the heart beats in rhythm, keeping everything in sync. It's where traditions mix like ingredients in a family recipe, blending the old with the new, much like how a heart carries the history of every breath taken before. For blended families, the kitchen is more than a place to cook; it's a space of fusion, where past family traditions are honored, and new ones are created, seasoned with patience, understanding, and love.

The Brady Bunch, one of television's most iconic blended families, shows the kitchen's power as a gathering place for connection and tons of heart. In nearly every episode, family members converged in the kitchen to talk, work through disagreements, and bond over meals. The backdrop of the kitchen was a place for cooking, but at the forefront were heartfelt conversations, sibling rivalries, and moments of laughter—whether it was Carol Brady dishing out motherly advice as bacon sizzles, Alice providing comic relief, or Mike and the kids sorting through their differences over breakfast. Though scripted, their kitchen reflects a truth: it's where blended families find common ground, forging bonds over shared meals. While real-life blended families don't always wrap up conflicts within 30 minutes, the concept remains the same: the kitchen is where love is exchanged, and relationships are strengthened. Your family can create this circulation of vitality, too.

In this chapter, you'll learn to transform your kitchen using Feng Shui to optimize energy flow and life coaching to foster collaboration. These tools will make your blended family's kitchen a heart that nourishes body, soul, and connection, fortifying unity and joy.

Why the kitchen matters

The kitchen is your home's vital core, where meals and memories nourish relationships. Its energy shapes how families interact—whether they linger to share stories or scatter with plates in hand. It's a place where morning conversations begin over coffee, where kids excitedly share stories from their day while grabbing an afternoon snack, and where dinner becomes a ritual of reconnection rather than just another task. In Feng Shui, the kitchen governs abundance and health, its chi flowing freely when organized and warm. A cluttered or divisive kitchen stifles connection, leaving interactions rushed or tense.

Blended families face unique challenges in the kitchen. Differing traditions—one parent's home-cooked dinners versus another's takeout nights—can spark friction. Stepchildren may feel out of place if meal routines favor one household's habits, like strict table times versus casual snacking. Cluttered counters or unequal chores breed resentment, making the kitchen a chore zone rather than a haven. These tensions disrupt the heart's rhythm, weakening family bonds, leaving behind disconnection or bitterness.

A connected kitchen offers a solution. Inclusive rituals, like shared meal prep, signal belonging, which unites stepchildren and parents. The kitchen should be a space where everyone, from toddlers to teens to adults, feels welcome and motivated to participate in the act of nourishing both the body and the soul. A Feng Shui-inspired layout—clear counters, a vibrant stove—enhances vitality and harmony. Involving kids in cooking or table-setting fosters teamwork, easing transitions between homes. This transformation turns the kitchen into a hub where blended families craft new traditions, from taco nights to heartfelt talks. Like a heart sustaining life, a connected kitchen nourishes unity. It reduces conflict and fosters joy, making every meal a step toward togetherness.

A worldwide look back

Cultures have long crafted kitchens as communal hearts, cultivating concord and tradition, offering wisdom for blended families. These spaces were designed to unite, much like today's kitchens.

In ancient Rome, the *culina* was the center of household life. Clay ovens glowed as families gathered, dipping bread in olive oil, discussing politics, trade, and the events of the day. Imagine the rich aroma of herbs and roasted meats, tables set for all. Cooking wasn't just a task; it was an experience, a communal effort that reinforced relationships and the importance of togetherness. This collective spirit inspires blended families to create inclusive kitchen spaces where conversation flows.

In many African cultures, communal cooking has long been a bonding experience. Food preparation was an activity where multiple generations contributed. One person ground spices, another stirred the pot, and children eagerly participated, learning the skills and wisdom passed down through storytelling. This hands-on approach motivates blended families to invite every family member—regardless of age or background—to take part in meal preparation, reinforcing the idea that everyone fits into the family.

These historical examples highlight the kitchen's role as a unifying hub. For blended families, embracing this mindset can help create new traditions that unite all family members, making the kitchen a place of warmth and belonging.

The energy behind the kitchen

During the spring of 2020, as the world came to a standstill, my husband discovered a new skill that would transform the energy of our home—he learned to cook. Like many others during the pandemic, he picked up something that had been dormant, a necessity turned passion. However, on top of making meals he unknowingly shifted the energy of our blended family dynamic.

At that time, our household was busier than ever. My stepson, home from college, studied online; my other stepson tackled virtual high school; our daughter navigated kindergarten over little boxes on a computer screen. It was messy, it was challenging, it was chaotic—it was our new normal. Everyone was home except my husband, who had the unique opportunity to go to the office. Without the usual traffic, he made it home much quicker, and that's when everything shifted.

I needed a break. Between homeschooling, managing the household, figuring out how to work remotely, and trying to maintain a sense of balance, I was stretched thin. That's when my husband took on cooking for our family. It was a beautiful gift, not just because it took something off my plate, but because of the energy shift it created. While he experimented with the pressure cooker (his new favorite appliance), I was able to take walks, practice yoga, and carve out time for myself. As he prepped meals, the boys joined, and soon the kitchen became a place of curiosity and creativity rather than just another chore-filled space.

Every evening, when we sat down for dinner, there was a collective exhale. Despite the chaos outside and the uncertainty of the world, we had this moment when our old normal blended with our new normal. The kitchen became our refuge, our constant. It was the one place where we could momentarily forget about everything else and just be together.

When a kitchen is energetically balanced, it fosters a sense of security and peace. For blended families, where multiple histories, routines, and expectations merge, ensuring that the kitchen remains a space of comfort and connection is essential. Whether it's through the simple act of cooking together, designating meal prep responsibilities, or creating a cozy and inviting dining area, the kitchen has the power to bring families together in a way that few other spaces can.

The energy behind the kitchen is not just about the food; it's about the way it makes you feel. And when you infuse it with intention, warmth, and love, it becomes more than a room; it becomes the heart of your home.

The science of mealtime connection

Research shows kitchen design and shared meals impact family dynamics. A connected kitchen fosters communication and well-being, vital for blended families.

- **Meals strengthen communication.**[26] A study from the *Journal of Family Psychology* reports that families who eat together regularly have stronger communication skills and better conflict resolution. Shared dinners unite blended families in understanding.

- **Mealtimes boost kids' confidence.**[27] Research from the *Pediatrics* journal states that children in families that prioritize mealtimes report higher self-esteem and lower rates of anxiety and depression. Mealtimes nurture the emotional health of kids in blended families.

- **Eating together fosters healthier habits.**[28] A study from the *American Journal of Clinical Nutrition* reveals that families who share meals tend to consume more nutritious foods. Blended families build lifelong healthy habits together.

- **Designed spaces deepen bonds.**[29] Research from the *Journal of Family Psychology* finds that families who eat together in a space designed for connection report they feel closer. Connection-focused spaces reduce arguments, fostering closeness in stepfamilies.

These findings highlight that a connected kitchen nurtures unity and joy. Let's explore practical steps to create this space.

How to create a kitchen that encourages connection

Constructing a connected kitchen blends Feng Shui's vibrant energy with life coaching's collaborative spirit. These steps, which can be done in any order, nourish family bonds:

1. **Involve everyone in meal preparation:** Assign small, age-appropriate kitchen tasks to each family member to imbue a sense of empowerment. Even young children can stir ingredients, while older kids can chop vegetables or set the table.

2. **Honor the stove:** Clean the stove regularly, as it represents wealth in Feng Shui. Position it to face the room's entrance or add a reflective element so the cook can see outwards, enhancing prosperity and vitality.

3. **Use warm lighting:** Install dimmable lights or pendants. Overhead lights, pendant lamps, or even candles enhance the ambience, making the kitchen feel cozy and welcoming.

4. **Display meaningful items:** Incorporate personal touches like a recipe board, chalkboard messages of encouragement, or heirloom cookbooks. Let kids contribute décor ideas for ownership. These make the kitchen feel like a shared space rather than just a functional one.

5. **Minimize clutter to promote flow:** A cluttered kitchen can feel chaotic and unwelcoming, stifling the flow of chi. Keep countertops clear, organize pantry items, and make sure frequently used utensils and appliances are easily accessible.

6. **Be mindful of seating arrangements:** In Feng Shui, round or oval tables encourage inclusivity, while square or rectangular tables should have balanced seating to avoid a feeling of hierarchy. Ensuring that everyone has a designated seat helps children feel a sense of belonging.

7. **Create rituals around mealtime:** Establish traditions that make mealtimes special, such as "Taco Tuesdays," breakfast for dinner every Sunday, or a gratitude practice where everyone shares one highlight from their day before eating.

These steps make your kitchen a pulsing heart, fostering connection. By making thoughtful changes to your kitchen, you can transform it from just a functional space into a gathering place that boosts blended family ties.

Client Case Study

One blended family I coached struggled with kitchen tension. The couple had married later in life and didn't have children together, which created a unique set of family dynamics. She felt disconnected when her husband's adult children visited their cozy townhome. Conversations were strained, and the energy was heavy—the exact opposite of their lively restaurant meetups. She sensed an energetic block but couldn't pinpoint why.

During the consultation, I noted the kitchen's indulgent cues: liquor bottles and cocktail photos, along with cookie jars, pastries, and bowls of candy that spilled into the adjacent family room. These all misaligned with the stepchildren's sobriety and clean-eating habits. The cramped dining table, set for two, felt exclusive. In Feng Shui, a kitchen's energy shapes interactions; this one signaled disconnect.

I explained how Feng Shui teaches us that our surroundings impact our emotions and interactions. If a space is filled with visual cues that don't resonate with those who enter, it can create subconscious resistance. With this realization, my client made some subtle but powerful changes that included:

- **Balancing visual energy:** She moved the alcohol collection to a closed cabinet rather than prominently displaying it. The wine and cocktail artwork was replaced with neutral décor that reflected nature scenes they too enjoyed.

- **Introducing healthier visual cues:** While she and her husband still enjoyed their treats, she placed fresh fruit in bowls on the counter and incorporated a tea station that felt more inviting to all—something that also helped kick their sweet habit.

- **Adjusting the seating layout:** The kitchen had a small dining table with two seats. She expanded the seating to make it feel more welcoming for visitors, ensuring they had a comfortable place to gather.

The transformation was profound. The next time her stepchildren visited, the conversations flowed easily, and their stay lasted much longer than usual. The energy in the space felt lighter, and she noticed that everyone seemed more relaxed and comfortable. The kitchen became the heart of connection, and in turn, their relationships deepened. At their next holiday gathering, her stepchildren stayed twice as long as usual—a shift she directly linked to the more inclusive energy in the space.

This reset shows blended families that a kitchen's energy shapes relationships. In blended families, where histories and lifestyles often differ, ensuring that the kitchen reflects balance and inclusivity can transform the space for all.

Did You Know?

- *Families who eat at least four meals together per week report feeling more connected and engaged.*

- *The color red is believed to stimulate appetite, which is why many restaurants use it in their branding.*

- *Kitchens with open shelving often encourage family members to participate more in cooking and meal prep.*

- *Playing soft background music while cooking can elevate mood and make the experience more enjoyable.*

Your Turn

The kitchen is where connection, laughter, and shared experiences come naturally, the heart that continues to beat all on its own. Let intention guide you toward a space where your blended family thrives by following these reflective steps.

Mantra: *"When we nourish the body, we nourish the soul."* Food is more than sustenance; it's a ritual of care and a reflection of love.

1. **Assess your kitchen:** Walk through your kitchen and consider what energy it holds. Does it feel inviting? Does it encourage connection? Is it cluttered or unwelcoming? Why?

2. **Make one small change:** Whether it's decluttering, adding a communal seating area, or establishing a mealtime ritual. Which one change can you implement this week? How does the kitchen feel afterward?

3. **Involve the whole family:** Encourage family members to contribute to meals, set the table, or suggest new traditions. Instead of assigning tasks, ask each person how they want to contribute. How does their input shift the family dynamics?

4. **Set a goal:** Picture your ideal kitchen vibe. What adjectives come to mind? What steps will get you there?

Reflect and Record Your Progress: After one week of creating a connected kitchen, write down one or more positive changes in its energy or family interactions (e.g., "*All our kids are helping with meal prep and we're laughing more during dinners*"). How does the space feel different? Have you noticed more family members naturally gathering? How can this reset become a family cornerstone?

A strong heart keeps a body thriving, in the same way a warm and welcoming kitchen keeps a family beating as one. Every step creates a space where unity grows.

Chapter 8

CREATING POSITIVE RITUALS

HOW INTENTIONAL ACTS NURTURE CONNECTION IN BLENDED FAMILY TRADITIONS

"Rituals are the formulas by which harmony is restored."
—Terry Tempest Williams

R ituals are the threads weaving a blended family's tapestry, delicate yet strong, binding diverse histories into a vibrant whole. Like a quilt stitched from varied fabrics—some inherited, some newly chosen—these acts blend old traditions with fresh patterns to create accord. The beauty of this quilt isn't in its uniformity but in its diversity, where every thread, whether innate or newly formed, contributes to the strength and warmth of the whole. In a blended family, rituals are vital, intertwining separate pasts into a shared present, their repetition strengthening bonds. A thoughtful ritual fosters connection; a neglected one frays the fabric, leaving gaps of disconnection.

The Kardashian-Jenners—a modern blended dynasty—embody the power of rituals. Their lavish annual Christmas Eve party is a hallmark of their family identity. The air buzzes with excitement as beautifully dressed guests step into a space filled with twinkling lights, sparkling décorations, and the scent of pine mingling with freshly baked cookies. Long tables are adorned with elegant centerpieces, and laughter echoes through the halls as family and friends come together to celebrate. These moments unite their sprawling clan, from Kris's kids to Caitlyn's and beyond. This party is a thoughtful act of connection, bringing together people from different dynamics and backgrounds to affirm their unity as a family. Even beyond grand celebrations, the Kardashians prioritize smaller, everyday rituals. Picture family dinners where voices overlap in animated conversation, or their weekly check-ins that keep them connected amidst their whirlwind schedules. These acts, grand or simple, weave their family's tapestry, showing blended families that intentional rituals create belonging. Your family can stitch this unity, too.

In this chapter, you'll learn to craft rituals using Feng Shui to shift energy and to foster inclusion using life coaching strategies. These tools will transform your blended family's traditions into a tapestry of connection, nurturing stability, joy, and a shared identity.

Why rituals matter

Rituals are the warp and weft of family life, providing structure and stability, especially in blended families navigating new modifications. They create predictable moments—bedtime stories, holiday feasts—that ground children and parents alike, signaling belonging. Rituals in Feng Shui are essential because they shift the chi energy and create balance in your space. Just as clutter or stagnation can block positive energy, mindful rituals help clear, activate, and invite fresh, beneficial chi into your home and life. Without them, families risk disconnection, their days chaotic and filled with separation.

Blended families face unique ritual challenges. Stepchildren may cling to old traditions from one household or resist new ones, creating tension. Parents might struggle to blend differing practices—formal dinners versus casual brunches—leaving some feeling excluded. Inconsistent rituals can deepen divides, making stepchildren feel like guests rather than family. It's also important to know it's okay for different households to have different rituals. If children split time, each home should have its own traditions that strengthen the bonds within that environment. It's not about competing, rather, about creating meaningful connections in both places, like a woven tapestry.

Intentional rituals offer a solution. Shared acts, like a weekly game night, knit everyone into the family's fabric, fostering ownership. Feng Shui-inspired rituals, such as lighting a candle at dinner to invite warmth can also set intentions of connectedness and help clear negative energy. Involving all members in creating traditions—kids picking a holiday dish or parents leading a gratitude practice—builds a shared identity. For children, these rituals can serve as emotional touchpoints, giving them something to look forward to and rely on. For parents, they offer an opportunity to lead by example, demonstrating love, patience, and inclusion. These acts bridge the past and present to help create a shared identity. Instead of focusing on the differences between biological and stepfamily dynamics, rituals highlight the unity of the household. They say, "*This is who we are, together.*" Like a quilt's stitches, rituals strengthen connection. They reduce anxiety and nurture joy, crafting a home where every thread counts.

A worldwide look back

Cultures have long used rituals to interlace communal bonds, offering wisdom for blended families. These acts were designed to unite, much like today's family traditions.

In Indigenous cultures, rituals often revolved around nature, like fire rituals to foster community. Envision a circle of people seated around a crackling blaze, the hypnotic flames blending with the rhythmic beat of drums, as sacred herbs burned to cleanse negative energy. These ceremonies passed down wisdom, teaching younger generations about respect and interconnectedness. This inspires blended families to create grounding rituals, like a weekly gratitude circle, uniting generations.

Similarly, in ancient Rome, families gathered daily around the household hearth to honor the *Lares*—guardian spirits believed to protect the home and family. Imagine soft prayers murmured and the firelight warming faces, as daily offerings affirmed lineage. This daily ritual sought protection and affirmed family links to their ancestors, creating a lineage of love and care. This practice encourages blended families to craft daily rituals, like a pre-dinner blessing, to anchor connection and honor shared history.

For blended families, these historical examples offer inspiration. Like the communal fire or the shared hearth, rituals can become the interwoven threads of the home, constructing a cover that brings everyone together.

The energy behind rituals

As a new mom in a blended family, I learned about the energy of rituals through our daughter. My husband's ex-wife, whom our daughter calls "Auntie," has been a wonderful part of our lives. Whenever my husband and I travel, she watches our daughter, embodying the nurturing qualities we're so grateful for in her. I remember one of the first trips where we left our daughter at Auntie's house. Her golden doodle greeted us at the door, full of energy as a long-lost friend. As we said goodbye, I felt a twinge of guilt—questioning my part in disrupting her sense of security—along with so many other limiting and insecure thoughts.

In those early days of motherhood, I believed every detail of my daughter's bedtime routine had to be meticulously followed for her to feel safe and secure. I would write down minute-by-minute itineraries, thinking this ritual would ensure comfort while Mom and Dad were away. One day, my daughter casually mentioned that bedtime at Auntie's house was different, still cozy and comforting, but not what Mommy does. In that moment, I realized I had a choice. I could insist that Auntie follow my detailed routine, or I could embrace the idea that my daughter could thrive with two different bedtime rituals. I chose the latter. Not only did it strengthen our daughter's adaptability, but it also reinforced the positive energy and trust between our two households. Our daughter's ease, giggling in both homes, showed the power of rituals to blend families. The energy was transformative. Tensions eased, trust grew, and our village strengthened. Over time, this realization reinvented the way we approached other rituals in our family.

This experience reminded me that rituals aren't about rigid control; they're about creating the right energy, love, and connection for your family. Just as the boys have two moms to guide and nurture them, our daughter now has a bonus mom of her own in Auntie. Blended families can weave these threads, fostering connection across households. It's this energy of support, inclusiveness, and flexibility that families need to strive for in the home. Rituals don't have to look the same everywhere; they just have to reflect the love and intention you want to share.

The science of rituals

Research shows rituals shape emotional and social well-being. They anchor blended families by intertwining stability and connection in various scientific ways.

- **Routines lower stress.**[30] Research conducted in *Psychoneuroendocrinology* finds that daily rituals reduce cortisol, helping participants feel calmer and more grounded. Intentional acts soothe blended family tensions.

- **Rituals build closeness.**[31] A study from the *Psychological Science* journal shows that shared rituals enhance feelings of closeness and cooperation within groups. Family formalities strengthen stepfamily bonds.

- **Rituals signal stability.**[32] In a study published in *Neuroscience Letters*, neuroscientists reported that daily rituals create neural pathways that signal safety and stability. Small acts of intention reinforce a sense of security and emotional grounding within blended families.

- **Gratitude boosts joy.**[33] Research in the *Journal of Personality and Social Psychology* finds that practicing gratitude rituals is linked to higher levels of life satisfaction and emotional resilience. Blended families thrive with thankful practices.

These findings highlight that rituals weave unity and resilience, fostering a healthier, happier household. Understanding the psychological and emotional impact of rituals is just the beginning. Let's explore practical steps to create positive, lasting rituals in your own blended family.

How to create positive rituals

Crafting rituals blends Feng Shui's energy-clearing power with life coaching's inclusive focus. These steps weave a tapestry of connection that aligns with your family's unique dynamic:

1. **Start small:** To build consistency, begin with a simple ritual that feels natural. It could be a nightly gratitude circle, a weekend game night, or a weekly call to extended family.

2. **Make it inclusive:** Ensure that the ritual involves everyone in the household, so all feel valued. For example, during a family meal, ask each person to share a highlight of their day.

3. **Tie it to existing habits:** For seamless integration, link the ritual to something you already do, like incorporating a short mindfulness moment before dinner or saying a family affirmation before bed.

4. **Clear the energy:** Use Feng Shui rituals, like burning sage or ringing a bell, to cleanse negativity before family gatherings. Add a clear quartz crystal to the ritual area to enhance the energy.

5. **Be consistent:** Rituals become meaningful through repetition. Choose a time and place that works for your family and stick to it as much as possible for continued momentum.

6. **Celebrate milestones:** Use rituals to mark special occasions or achievements, such as a family "first day of school" photo or a celebratory meal at your family's favorite restaurant when someone accomplishes a goal, which honors family growth.

7. **Adapt as needed:** Rituals should evolve with your family to stay mean-

ingful and relevant. Be open to suggestions from all members, ensuring that the practices continue to feel pertinent and engaging.

Rituals progress with time, just as blended families do. By intentionally crafting moments that feel both familiar and inclusive, you create a foundation where every family member feels valued and connected.

Client Case Study

When I first met my client, she and her husband had just moved from the state where she had grown up and raised her family. The move was for a beautiful reason—to be closer to her son, who was expecting his first child—but despite the joy that came with this new chapter, she felt unsettled and emotionally adrift.

Her home didn't feel like her own yet. The furniture was arranged, the walls were painted, and the décor was carefully selected, yet something was missing. From the way she spoke, I sensed that this move hadn't been entirely her decision. There was an unspoken grief beneath her words, a quiet longing for the familiarity of the home and stepdaughter she had left behind.

But the moment she talked about her soon-to-arrive grandchild, everything changed. Her posture lifted, her eyes sparkled with excitement, and her voice carried a warmth that had been absent before. That was when I knew that her heart wasn't stuck in the past; it simply needed a bridge to the present. And that bridge would be built through rituals.

Together, we started small. If this home was going to feel like her own, it needed to tell her family's story. We began with the young grandchild's room—not just a spare bedroom but a place of invitation, comfort, and familiarity. Cozy touches were added to create nightly rituals of bedtime stories and morning routines filled with music. Family heirlooms were hung in the hallway. Her expression shifted as each piece was placed. The home was becoming a place where memories would be made. There was still one final touch to be done: setting intentions for outdoor traditions. She loved the idea and already planned for annual family photos taken against the panoramic mountain views.

Then the most surprising shift happened. Her stepdaughter, who had once seemed hesitant about this new chapter, moved to the same state. It was the power of family rituals: the quiet, steady rhythm of belonging she had witnessed in her parents' home, which she craved to be near again. It was a reminder that home isn't just a place; it's energy, a feeling, a tempo that we create over time.

Through the process of intentionally creating rituals, my client didn't just adjust to a new home; she embraced it, infused it with life, and turned it into a haven. The rituals she built, like bedtime storytelling and seasonal photo traditions, have become beloved cornerstones for both her grandchildren and stepdaughter alike. The place was no longer just walls and furniture, but a home that would be passed down through generations—a foundation of connection, laughter, and belonging.

Did You Know?

- *Morning rituals, like a shared breakfast or a family affirmation, can set a positive tone for the entire day.*

- *Simple rituals, such as lighting a candle during family discussions, can signal mindfulness and create a calming atmosphere.*

- *Even a 15-minute family walk after dinner can become a cherished ritual that promotes both connection and health.*

- *Smiling changes your brain chemistry. Even if you don't feel happy at first, smiling as a morning and evening ritual can shift your energy and improve your mood.*

Your Turn

Rituals weave your blended family's tapestry, creating stability and joy. Start with intention, then follow these steps, and let purpose guide you toward traditions that prosper.

Mantra: "*When we honor traditions, we strengthen our bonds.*" Rituals are the thread that holds families together. Create them with joy.

1. **Reflect on your family's needs:** What moments of connection are missing from your routine? What rituals could help fill those gaps?

2. **Start rituals of your own:** Are there any old traditions from your past that you'd like to reintroduce or modify for your blended family? What new rituals can you introduce that feel authentic to your current family dynamic?

3. **Get everyone involved:** If you were to envision your family five years from now, what meaningful traditions would you like to see in place?

How would each family member answer?

4. **Make small strides:** What small moments in your daily routine already feel like rituals? How do they impact your family's sense of connection?

Reflect and Record Your Progress: After a month of implementing a ritual, write down one or more positive changes in your family's energy or interactions (e.g., "*Our family game nights spark laughter like never before*"). How have these practices shifted the energy in your home? What new traditions are emerging? How can these rituals become your family's legacy?

Rituals—whether as simple as a compliment to start the day or as elaborate as a holiday tradition—are the threads that weave your family together. Every step creates a tapestry of harmony.

Chapter 9

BRIDGING DIFFERENCES WITH SHARED GOALS

HOW TO HONOR DIFFERENT STYLES, BACKGROUNDS, & PERSONALITIES IN DESIGN

"Love builds bridges where there are none."
—R.H. Delaney

B lended families are like bridges built with patience and strengthened by a collective purpose. Each family member stands on their own shore, bringing unique histories, traditions, and emotions. At first, the distance may seem vast, the waters beneath uncertain. However, when we commit to building a bridge together, step by step, plank by plank, a path toward connection is constructed. The foundation is laid with respect, ensuring each person's voice is heard. The beams are reinforced with shared experiences, moments that unite us. And the strongest support comes from common goals, whether it's raising happy, well-adjusted children, creating a home filled with love, or simply choosing patience and kindness along the way.

Kurt Russell and Goldie Hawn, Hollywood's blended family icons, built such a bridge. When they came together, they each had children from previous relationships—Goldie's kids, Oliver and Kate Hudson, and Kurt's son, Boston Russell, and their son Wyatt Russell. Instead of forcing a traditional family mold, they chose a more fluid, intuitive approach, allowing relationships to develop organically and authentically. They understood that love isn't dictated by biology or choosing sides but by the care, respect, and intentional effort we put into relationships. Goldie has spoken about making the world a better place through parental influence and putting love back into the children we raise, blood or not. Decades later, they remain one of Hollywood's most admired families, proving that bridging differences isn't about removing individuality; it's about finding ways to coexist in harmony.

In this chapter, you'll learn to align your home with shared goals using coaching strategies to foster communication and collaboration, and Feng Shui to balance energy. These tools will bridge differences, creating a space that honors independence while nurturing connection, unity, and love in your blended family.

Why aligning your space with shared goals matters

The physical environment of your home has a profound impact on how family members feel and interact with one another. Your home reflects your family's collective energy, interactions, and overall well-being. When a home exhibits balance and inclusiveness, it naturally fosters connection and harmony. But when differences in style, function, or traditions are left unaddressed, they can lead to feelings of disconnection, frustration, or even resentment.

Blended families face unique design hurdles when mingling goals. Stepchildren may feel like guests if spaces echo one parent's past but not their present. Parents might clash over aesthetics—one's minimalist vibe versus another's cozy clutter—causing friction. Differing routines, like strict chore schedules versus relaxed ones, can make shared goals feel divisive. Without a joint vision, the home becomes a patchwork of "yours" and "mine," not a cohesive bridge to "ours."

Just like yin and yang, opposing forces are not meant to compete but to complement each other, creating a stronger, more balanced whole. Aligning spaces with shared goals transforms the blended family vibe. Life coaching tools, like family vision-setting, clarify collective aspirations into a home where everyone feels valued. Feng Shui's balanced layouts, like neutral communal areas, promote inclusive chi flow. Involving all members in design choices and goal-setting—for instance, parents scheduling quality family time on the command center, or kids picking where the command center is hung—builds ownership mixed with collectivism, easing transitions between households. This alignment weaves differences into a unified home, making every space a step toward togetherness. Like a bridge spanning shores, a shared vision connects the hearts of your blended family.

A worldwide look back

Across cultures, homes have always evolved to reflect the people who live in them. Blended families can elicit motivation from history, designing spaces that honor their shared identity while allowing each person's individuality to shine.

In traditional Japanese households, rooms were designed with flexibility in mind. *Shoji screens* allowed spaces to transform based on daily activities, so that the household could shift the space as needed. The minimalist aesthetic highlighted this balance. Picture tatami mats and natural light filtering through paper screens to create a serene environment. This adaptability inspires blended families to create fluid spaces that evolve with everyone's needs, fostering inclusion.

In Scandinavian culture, the concept of *hygge* is a way to cultivate warmth, harmony, and emotional connection within the home. More than just cozy décor, hygge is a shared mindset, one that values presence, comfort, and intentional togetherness. Visualize a Nordic family gathered around wooden tables to share meals, stories, and laughter, with flickering candlelight that made everyone feel included and safe. This mindset encourages blended families to design cozy, neutral spaces—like a communal nook—that prioritize emotional unity over stylistic divides.

Throughout history, homes have reflected the families who lived in them, evolving with the needs of those under one roof. These traditions highlight homes as bridges of connection.

The energy behind bridging differences

My husband and I don't argue often, perhaps because he was raised in a family that openly discussed everything, or maybe because of my undergraduate and graduate degrees in communication. But we are human, and like any couple, we have moments of conflict. One of our personal rules is to never go to bed angry, but sometimes that's easier said than done. I remember one argument in particular; actually, I don't even remember what it was about, but I do recall the way it felt. That night, we broke our own rule and went to bed upset.

The next morning, the energy in the house was different. Have you ever felt that? That heavy, stagnant air, where unspoken words seem to linger? Science teaches us that emotions carry energy, much like radio waves that travel unseen but can still be heard and, in this case, felt. Negative emotions have a frequency, and when left unresolved, they can settle into the structures that bridge the home and its people.

By morning, we both knew that something had to shift. Oddly enough, I'm grateful that my husband went through a divorce because, during couples counseling, he learned conflict resolution strategies that aren't commonly taught in school. Through my own education and experience teaching conflict management at the college level, I also gained valuable tools. Together, we've learned to approach conflict not as something to win, but rather as something to navigate with intention and respect.

Here are some coaching strategies we use to resolve conflicts and maintain the positive and uplifting energy in our home:

1. **Pause:** Give yourself time to process emotions before responding. Reacting out of anger only deepens the divide. Also, communicate if you need a break to clear your mind, which helps prevent unnecessary escalation.

2. **Use "I" statements:** Instead of saying, "*You never listen to me*," try, "*I feel unheard when we don't discuss things together*." This shifts the focus from blame to understanding.

3. **Find common ground:** What's the shared goal? Whether it's making the home feel more in accord or ensuring everyone feels included, focusing on common ground helps ease tension.

4. **Release the ego:** At the core of many conflicts is the need to be "right." When we let go of our ego and prioritize the relationship, resolution comes much faster.

5. **Express appreciation:** After a conflict is resolved, affirm your commitment to the relationship. A simple "*I appreciate you*" can reset the energy in the home.

Every choice we make, especially in our relationships, has a ripple effect on the energy of our home. By choosing communication, patience, and mutual respect, we create an environment that supports love and connection. Blended families can bridge differences in a similar way, using shared goals to align spaces and hearts.

The science of home energy and connection

Research shows home design and shared goals shape family dynamics. Aligned spaces promote interconnection and well-being, vital for blended families.

- **Design boosts cohesion.**[34] According to a study from the *Journal of Environmental Psychology*, homes that are designed to facilitate conversation and shared experiences improve family cohesion. Blended families connect in spaces built for togetherness.

- **Personalization fosters belonging.**[35] Research from the *Family Relations* journal reveals that families who collaborate on home design decisions tend to experience a stronger sense of unity and shared purpose. Co-creating spaces bonds stepfamilies emotionally.

- **"Third spaces" bridge gaps.**[36] According to a study from the *Journal of Environmental Psychology*, neutral areas within the home (aka "third spaces"), like a reading nook, can help bridge differences. These neutral spaces create areas where blended family members naturally connect.

- **Consciousness elevates joy.**[37] In the book *Power vs. Force,* David R. Hawkins describes states of consciousness on a scale from 1 to 1,000. Individuals who raise their consciousness above 200, toward levels like acceptance (350), love (500), and peace (600), experience greater happiness, health, and life fulfilment. Higher consciousness levels enrich blended family harmony.

These findings highlight that aligned homes bridge differences, nurturing love. Let's explore practical steps to create these goals and designs.

How to align your space with shared goals

Aligning your home with shared goals is like building a bridge—each choice a plank toward unity. Life coaching fosters collaboration through open communication and vision-setting, while Feng Shui balances energy with thoughtful design, creating a space where differences harmonize. These steps build a home that reflects your blended family's collective vision:

1. **Set a family vision:** To foster inclusivity, hold a family meeting to define shared goals. Use life coaching's "I" statements (e.g., "*I want our space to feel welcoming*") to honor all voices, ensuring everyone feels heard. Write down the vision to solidify commitment.

2. **Blend aesthetics:** To unite diverse styles, create integrated spaces that reflect each member's taste. Combine a kid's vibrant painting with a parent's sleek lamp in a living room, crafting a shared aesthetic. This collaborative design builds ownership and visual harmony.

3. **Balance energy:** To promote equilibrium, use Feng Shui to position furniture symmetrically, like equal seating in communal areas, ensuring chi to flow smoothly. Place a jade plant in a shared space to enhance unity and abundance, grounding the environment.

4. **Track progress:** To visualize growth, display a family milestone board with photos or notes of shared wins, like a group hike or a new décor project. This tangible reminder reinforces your bridge's strength, celebrating collective progress.

5. **Communicate openly:** To maintain alignment, schedule weekly check-ins to address tensions, focusing on common ground with open-ended questions drawn from coaching techniques (e.g., *"What makes our home feel united?"*). This practice nurtures collective trust.

6. **Celebrate milestones:** To reinforce unity, mark family wins with shared activities, like a dinner or game night. These celebrations honor the journey, strengthening your bridge with joy and togetherness.

Just as every bridge requires maintenance to remain strong, so does the emotional infrastructure of your home. These steps build a solid foundation of connection, honoring differences while establishing a unified home.

Client Case Study

One couple reached out after completing a full remodeling of their home. They requested an energetic space clearing to refresh the energy after months of construction. The home itself was pristine—every corner styled with intention, every surface immaculate. They welcomed me warmly and appeared happy, but as I moved through their home with sage in hand, I sensed something deeper.

The primary bedroom carried a noticeable weight. The air felt dense, almost sorrowful, despite the beauty of the space. Trusting my intuition, I gently asked how things were going in their marriage. The wife exhaled with visible relief and shared that, while she loved her husband deeply, she felt like she'd been silently holding everything together. She didn't want to add to his stress, especially as he was managing work and extended family pressures.

Later, as I cleared the husband's home office, he opened up as well—he missed the intimacy they once shared but admitted their relationship had fallen to the bottom of the priority list.

Two rooms. Two stories. One shared goal: reconnection.

I returned the next day with a full Feng Shui report and some coaching strategies. Together, we addressed both the physical layout and the emotional dynamics of their home:

- **Bedroom balance:** Their bed was pushed against one wall, subtly symbolizing imbalance. We centered it and added matching nightstands to reflect equality in the relationship.

- **Clearing stagnant energy:** Unfinished projects and visual clutter in their bedroom mirrored emotional buildup. We cleared the space and reset the intention for renewal.

- **Inviting connection:** His office was all business. We introduced elements for personal presence, like a cozy chair for shared conversations, along with meaningful family photos.

- **Sharing communication rituals:** We added weekly check-ins—short, intentional conversations about their relationship goals, focused on moving forward rather than rehashing the past.

Within weeks, they reported feeling lighter, not just in their home but with each other too. Months later, they described not only the stronger emotional connection but also a noticeable boost in productivity and intimacy, something they hadn't felt since the early years of their marriage.

This case study reflects a deeper truth: when a couple aligns their physical space with their shared goals, transformation unfolds. For blended families especially, designing a home with intention becomes a bridge—a way to honor individual paths while creating a future built together.

Did You Know?
- *Establishing shared goals increases family harmony. Psychology research suggests that families who set collective goals experience greater cohesion, mutual respect, and a deeper sense of belonging.*

- *Families who operate from elevated conscious states, such as love, gratitude, and understanding, experience healthier relationships. When a home is intentionally designed to support these elevated states, collective growth is infused.*

- *Writing down your goals increases success rates by 42%. This simple act turns an abstract wish into a tangible intention. Manifestation and goal-setting begin with clarity, and clarity is rooted in definition.*

Your Turn

Bridging differences in a blended family is like building a suspension bridge: each side starts from a different foundation, shaped by past experiences, goals, and perspectives. The strongest bridges are built with flexibility, allowing them to sway with the winds of change rather than break under pressure. Each step toward shared goals builds a pathway where love and unity thrive, honoring individuality while crafting a collective home.

Mantra: "*When we blend our spaces, we blend our stories.*" Every home tells a story, and this story can reflect the love and unity of building together.

1. **Assess the home together:** Walk through your home as a family and note which areas feel welcoming and which feel detached. Which spaces feel disconnected? Why?

2. **Define shared goals:** Have an open discussion about what you want your home to reflect and how it can better support your blended family dynamic. What shared vision unites your family? How can your home reflect it?

3. **Make one change:** Whether it's holding a vision talk or adding a milestone family photo wall, take a step toward creating a space that represents your collective goal. What small change could you make this week to enhance connections? How does it shift the energy?

4. **Celebrate together:** Acknowledge the progress you've made by planning a family activity to mark a shared goal win, whether it's a dinner, a movie night, or a shared creative project. What celebratory ideas can you come up with?

Reflect and Record Your Progress: After two weeks of aligning your home, write down one or more positive changes in its energy or family interactions (e.g., "*The living room feels like 'ours' now because we decorated it together*"). How does the space feel different? What new family goals are forming? How can this bridge become your family's legacy?

When your space aligns with your collective vision, your home becomes a refuge of connection, love, and unity—a bridge that binds. That's the beauty of a blended family: not where we began, but the bridge we build together.

Chapter 10

THE POWER OF ENERGETIC BOUNDARIES

How to Establish Energetic & Emotional Boundaries for Coherence

"Daring to set boundaries is about having the courage to love ourselves, even when we risk disappointing others."
—Brené Brown

Boundaries are like the banks of a river guiding a blended family's energy, channeling love and respect into a steady flow. Without them, emotions spill over, eroding trust and harmony; with them, relationships thrive, each member secure yet connected. In blended families, boundaries are vital, balancing individual needs with collective unity. Just as a river needs banks to define its course, family members need clear expectations and emotional guardrails to feel secure and valued. When boundaries are too rigid, the river runs dry, connection is lost, and relationships feel distant. But when boundaries are too loose, emotions flood unchecked, leading to tension, overwhelm, and exhaustion. With healthy boundaries in place, blended families can flow harmoniously with each person having space to be themselves while moving forward together.

Dwayne "The Rock" Johnson and his ex-wife, Dany Garcia, exemplify this balance. After their divorce, they redefined their riverbanks, choosing reciprocated respect and communal boundaries. Though their marriage ended in divorce, they fostered a mindset of collaboration over separation, not only for their daughter but also for their professional lives. Instead of focusing on the traditional divorce narrative of loss and division, they built a new way forward, redefining their relationship, with Dany continuing as Dwayne's business manager, guiding his career into one of the most successful in Hollywood. They also remained deeply involved as co-parents, maintaining a strong foundation for teamwork, along with personal and professional regard for the changing of boundaries. Their approach serves as a powerful reminder that choosing a mindset of cooperation, rather than conflict, can transform partnerships in unexpected ways.

In this chapter, you'll learn to set energetic and emotional boundaries using life coaching strategies to clarify needs, and Feng Shui to structure energy. These tools will transform your blended family's home into a harmonious river, where individuality and unity flow together, nurturing peace, respect, and love.

Why energetic boundaries matter

Boundaries define what's yours to carry, protecting emotional and energetic well-being. In blended families, where complex dynamics—stepchildren, ex-partners, in-laws—can blur lines, clear boundaries prevent burnout and solidify respect. Without them, resentment festers, draining the home's vitality. Boundaries aren't about exclusion; they're about creating clarity, like riverbanks guiding a stream.

Blended families face many unique boundary challenges. When stepparents overstep disciplinary roles or assert control, this can spark tension, alienating their stepchildren. Or intrusions like ex-partners dropping by unannounced or kids sharing rooms can erode personal space. Along with children struggling to integrate without disrupting existing sibling bonds, ultimately leading to them feeling like outsiders. Emotional exhaustion from balancing everyone's needs leaves parents depleted, their energy scattered. In Feng Shui, such imbalances block chi, making homes feel chaotic, heavy, or *off*, amplifying stress.

Strong boundaries offer a solution. Life coaching tools, like "I" statements (e.g., a stepparent saying, "*I need clear co-parenting guidelines*"), help clarify roles. Feng Shui's physical boundaries, like partitions or sacred spaces, protect chi flow, grounding the home. For stepchildren, defined spaces—like personal desks—signal belonging, which eases transition. For parents, saying no to over-involvement preserves energy and strengthens leadership. These boundaries channel emotions constructively, fostering coherence. Feng Shui teaches us that our environment reflects our internal state, so when we honor our boundaries, we cultivate balance, clarity, and empowerment in all areas of life.

Like a river's banks, boundaries guide connection. They reduce conflict and nurture trust, creating a home where energy flows smoothly. By setting strong energetic boundaries, you protect your peace, enhance your home's energy, and invite greater happiness into your life.

A worldwide look back

Cultures have long used boundaries to harmonize relationships, offering wisdom for blended families. These practices balanced individual and collective needs, much as in today's homes.

In India, the concept of *Lakshman Rekha* originates from the epic Ramayana. It symbolizes an invisible yet powerful boundary that protects one's personal space and well-being. Imagine a delicate line drawn around a sacred space, keeping unwanted energy out while maintaining peace within. For blended families, this metaphor is incredibly relevant in defining where your energy begins and ends, to ensure that external stressors don't seep into the riverbanks of your home.

In Maasai culture, *bomas* (traditional homesteads) are constructed in circular formations, each section designated for a specific family unit. The structure itself reflects an unspoken boundary that there is a place for everyone, but space must be respected and maintained for harmony to exist. This mirrors the dynamic of blended families, where each person must have their own emotional space while still contributing to the greater whole.

These cultural insights remind us that boundaries have always been essential for balance and connection—not as a way to exclude, but rather, as a way to create structure and emotional well-being. These traditions highlight boundaries as coherence-builders.

The energy behind boundaries

Early on in our relationship, my husband's ex-wife had the opportunity to go to Africa for two weeks. It was the longest stretch we'd ever had the boys on our own, and we were thrilled. While we'd always shared a respectful co-parenting dynamic, this was the first time I'd be stepping more fully into a primary caregiver role for my stepsons—and with that, our family boundaries would start to gently shift.

The timing coincided with a mom/son event at our youngest's elementary school. He was excited about the games and snacks, and many of his friends were attending with their moms. Under normal circumstances, this type of event felt outside of my role as a bonus mom. I had always respected the unspoken boundary of not overlapping too much with his mother's social circles. But this time was different. I chose to go—for him.

Walking into the brightly lit cafeteria, I was greeted by the sugary scent of cotton candy and the sounds of squealing kids. But beneath the cheerful buzz, I felt a wave of discomfort. The other moms smiled politely but kept their distance. I suddenly felt like I didn't belong. I clung to my stepson's hand, smiling through the awkwardness, until he eventually ran off to join his friends.

Just as I began retreating inward, a woman approached me with warmth and kindness. She introduced herself, welcomed me into her circle, and completely shifted the energy. Her small gesture dissolved the invisible wall I'd built around myself. In that moment, I realized something vital: boundaries aren't about exclusion, they're about self-awareness. As a bonus mom, I still had every right to love my stepson and experience bonding moments free of judgment. I had put so much pressure on making sure I wasn't intruding that I forgot that openness creates new pathways for relationships to grow.

As a life coach, I often help clients understand that boundaries are about honoring your energy while staying open to meaningful connection. You can hold space for yourself *and* make space for others. That mom didn't just open up conversation—she reminded me that boundaries, when flexible, can become bridges.

In Feng Shui, energetic boundaries are essential for maintaining balance in the home. Whether it's setting clear zones for personal reflection or symbolically placing a rug to define space, boundaries protect and nourish your emotional center.

Boundaries are something we often don't think about until we are forced to navigate them. For blended families, setting energetic and emotional boundaries is crucial for maintaining relationships and preserving our own sense of self. Boundaries are about finding balance, not shutting ourselves off and not overextending where it doesn't feel aligned. Sometimes, all it takes is one welcoming gesture to change everything.

The science of boundaries

Boundaries are not just emotional constructs; they have a measurable impact on our mental and physical health. Understanding the science behind boundaries can help blended families navigate complex dynamics with confidence and clarity.

- **Boundaries ease anxiety.**[38] A study published in the *Journal of Anxiety Disorders* reveals that strong boundaries reduce anxiety, improving emotional stability. Clear limits empower blended families to thrive.

- **Emotions are contagious.**[39] A study from the journal *Social Psychological and Personality Science* shows that humans subconsciously absorb the emotions of those around them—without boundaries, we can take on stress that isn't ours. Boundaries protect stepfamilies from absorbing external stress.

- **Tension disrupts sleep.**[40] Research from the *Journal of Clinical Sleep Medicine* finds unresolved family tension harms sleep, causing burnout. Boundaries foster restful blended homes.

- **Boundaries build trust.**[41] Research from the *Journal of Family Psychology* reveals that boundary-setting families enjoy fewer conflicts and deeper trust. Boundaries allow for healthier and more constructive communication among blended families.

However, knowing you need boundaries and actually enforcing them are two different things. It takes intentionality, practice, and sometimes, trial and error to set and maintain boundaries that work for everyone involved. Let's explore practical steps to set them.

How to set energetic boundaries

Setting boundaries blends life coaching's clarity with Feng Shui's structured energy, guiding your blended family's flow like riverbanks. These steps, completed in any order, foster respect and harmony, ensuring emotional and energetic coherence.

1. **Clarify your boundaries:** To protect your energy, identify what drains you. Journal these triggers to pinpoint needed boundaries, like limiting involvement in ex-partner talks. Reflect weekly to refine your clarity.

2. **Communicate with confidence:** To foster respect, use "I" statements—*"I need quiet time after work"*—to express boundaries calmly. Practice aloud to build confidence, ensuring your voice is firm yet compassionate, inviting understanding.

3. **Practice saying no without guilt:** To preserve well-being, decline tasks misaligned with your energy, like extra co-parenting duties. Saying no prioritizes self-care, freeing space for meaningful family moments without resentment.

4. **Create rituals for reinforcement:** To ground your energy, practice a ritual, like a quick meditation or journaling, before any tough talks. This signals self-respect, strengthening your riverbanks with intention.

5. **Set "energetic office hours":** Just as professionals have set work-ing hours, designate your own emotional availability hours. Let family members know when you are open to discussions and when you need time for yourself to reset and recharge.

6. **Use Feng Shui to create physical boundaries:** A well-placed book-shelf or partition, or even a strategically placed rug, can create energetic separation between different areas of the home, helping to establish emotional comfort zones.

7. **Construct a "sacred space":** Designate a corner of your home as a personal retreat, like a chair by the window or a quiet meditation area. This signals to your family that this is your space to renew your energy without interruption.

A river needs its banks to guide its course, and families need healthy boundaries to navigate the complexities of relationships without losing themselves in the process. These steps help define what's yours to carry and what isn't, allowing space for emotional balance, clear communication, and a sense of harmony to shape your home.

Client Case Study

One of my clients reached out with a tender concern—her son and daugh-ter-in-law had been trying to conceive, and she desperately wanted to support them. Her son already had a child from a previous relationship, making their journey not just about expanding their family, but also about navigating the layered dynamics of a blended one. A believer in energy work, she found herself in a delicate situation: her son was open to holistic ideas, but her daughter-in-law was more skeptical, dismissing anything "woo-woo." My client didn't want to overstep, but she also didn't want to take no action at all.

As we spoke, it became clear that her desire to help was rooted in love, but also in fear of crossing a line. She asked, "*Is there any way I can support them energetically, without making her uncomfortable?*" The answer was yes, through soft, subtle, and respectful energetic boundaries.

We created a plan that honored everyone's comfort levels and values:

1. **Symbolic gift giving:** Instead of suggesting a practice directly, she gifted items that symbolized fertility and beginnings—peonies for love, and pomegranates and avocados as nods to pregnancy seeds and new life.

2. **Earth elements for grounding:** We included Feng Shui recommendations like warm-toned pottery, rose quartz, and feminine textures—items she could gift naturally, infusing their space with grounding, stabilizing energy.

3. **Hosting with intention:** She invited them for meals at her home, where she created a cozy, loving environment filled with candlelight, music, and warmth, setting an energetic intention into the space beforehand without ever mentioning fertility.

4. **Private affirmations:** Honoring her own spiritual practice, she quietly spoke affirmations and blessings for their future—never aloud to them, but always with love and trust.

Months later, my client called with joyful news—they were expecting. She shared, *"I never pushed or interfered. I just held space, and maybe that was enough."*

This story reflects the delicate art of supporting with boundaries. In any family—especially blended ones—it's tempting to help in ways we understand best. But true support sometimes means honoring others' journeys while gently sharing your own light. Months later, she shared that her daughter-in-law had warmed up significantly, and their relationship now included regular visits and mutual appreciation, built on the foundation of quiet respect and trust. As this case shows, powerful transformation often happens not through control, but rather, through quiet intention and sacred restraint.

Did You Know?

- *Individuals with strong personal boundaries experience lower stress levels, better emotional resilience, and improved mental health.*

- *Designated personal areas within a home can significantly reduce conflict and improve relationships, making personal spaces matter.*

- *Contrary to popular belief, rather than pushing people away, saying "no" strengthens relationships and cultivates respect.*

- *People who struggle with boundary-setting often experience disrupted sleep due to emotional overstimulation and mental exhaustion.*

Your Turn

Boundaries are riverbanks, guiding your blended family's energy with clarity and love. Each step strengthens coherence, balancing individuality and unity in a harmonious flow.

Mantra: "*Boundaries are not barriers; they are the foundation of respect and trust.*" Healthy relationships thrive when we honor personal space and emotional well-being.

1. **Assess your boundaries:** Take a moment to reflect on boundaries. Are there any areas where you feel drained, overextended, or unheard? Why?

2. **Communicate your needs:** Choose one boundary you'd like to reinforce and practice communicating it using an "I" statement. Example: "*I need just a little bit of personal time to recharge after work before I engage in conversations about household tasks.*" How does this shift conversations and connections?

3. **Reinforce the home environment:** Use Feng Shui techniques to create physical and energetic boundaries. Where can you create this space? Does it enhance peace within yourself? Within your family?

4. **Observe the impact:** Over the next week, pay attention to how these shifts affect your relationships and emotional well-being. What's different? How can you continue to reinforce healthy boundaries without guilt or fear?

Reflect and Record Your Progress: Since the act of setting boundaries often takes time, after a couple of weeks, write down one or more positive changes in your home's energy or family interactions (e.g., "*I feel calmer saying no and now my step-kids respect me more*"). How does the space feel? What new trust is forming? How can these boundaries become your family's strength?

Remember, boundaries are a form of self-respect and self-care. Your home is a river, its energy guided by boundaries. The more you honor your personal energy, the more you empower yourself to create a home where love flows freely.

Chapter 11

FROM CHAOS TO CALM WITH MINDSET SHIFTS

HOW TO CULTIVATE A MINDSET THAT TRANSFORMS TRIALS INTO CHANCES

"When you change the way you look at things, the things you look at change."
—Wayne Dyer

A mindset shift is like adjusting the lens on a camera. At first, everything may appear blurry, distorted, or out of reach. But then, with a small twist of focus, the scene sharpens. Details emerge that you never noticed before, like opportunities, blessings, or even beauty in places you once overlooked. You haven't changed the landscape; you've just changed how you see it. That's the power of a mindset shift. In a blended family, this shift can be everything. Where you once saw division, you begin to see diversity. Where you once felt resistance, you start to feel resilience. Suddenly, you're no longer reacting from old beliefs; you're responding from a place of clarity and awareness.

When Gwyneth Paltrow and Chris Martin divorced in 2014, they introduced the now-famous phrase "conscious uncoupling." Rather than letting their separation become a source of bitterness or detachment, they committed to redefining and refocusing on what family meant. Gwyneth has since spoken about the emotional growth required to shift from a romantic partnership to a blended family rooted in friendship and co-parenting, and how an intentional mindset helped her embrace the transition with grace. In an interview, Gwyneth described their approach this way: *"Chris and I are in a lot of contact; it's a very close friendship, and we're very much a family—even though we're not a couple."* Their ability to spend holidays together, take family vacations, and attend events as a unified front is a testament to the power of a mindset rooted in emotional maturity. Their story shows that when we prioritize peace over pride, we don't separate, we evolve.

In this chapter, you'll learn to cultivate a transformative mindset using life coaching techniques to reframe thoughts and Feng Shui to align energy. Mindset isn't about pretending everything is perfect; it's about choosing what stays in focus and what fades into the background. These tools will shift your blended family's home from chaos to calm, fostering clarity, connection, and peace.

Why mindset shifts matter

Your mind is your most powerful tool. The way you interpret situations directly influences your emotions, reactions, and ultimately, your household interactions. Without conscious mindset shifts, stress and frustration can become the default mode of operating in a combined home. In blended families, where complex dynamics—stepchildren's transitions, ex-partner tensions, or differing routines—can spark chaos, how you think determines the level of harmony created. A reactive mindset fuels stress; a proactive one fosters calm.

Blended families face unique mindset hurdles. Feeling like an outsider—*"I'll never belong"*—isolates stepparents. Resisting change—*"It shouldn't be this hard"*—breeds frustration. Comparing your family to "normal" families or expecting perfection—*"Everyone must get along"*—sets unrealistic bars. Taking things personally—*"They don't like me because I'm not their biological parent or child"*—deepens divides. These thoughts, unchecked, create internal chaos, straining relationships and home energy.

Mindset shifts offer a solution. Life coaching tools, like gratitude or pausing before reacting, rewire responses, which in turn eases tension. In Feng Shui, a cluttered space mirrors a cluttered mind; decluttering counters or adding plants aligns chi with clarity. Involving kids in mindful practices, like sharing daily wins, fosters belonging and eases transition. A mindset shift creates the energetic permission for transformation to occur, both within and around you. It takes practice, conscious choices, and a willingness to see challenges as stepping stones. You're not a victim of your circumstances—you're an active co-creator of the energy you live in. These shifts transform chaos into opportunity, creating a home where connections translate into a beautiful masterpiece.

Your beliefs shape your space. When you shift your mindset from limitation to possibility, the energy in your home follows suit. Like a lens sharpening focus, a mindset shift reveals possibility. It reduces conflict and nurtures peace, aligning your home with love.

A worldwide look back

Throughout history, different cultures have embraced mindset shifts as a way to adapt to life's challenges and cultivate resilience. People have long understood that how we perceive our circumstances determines our ability to navigate them with grace and strength.

In ancient Stoic philosophy, the concept of *amor fati* ("love of fate") encouraged people to embrace life's challenges. Envision a Roman philosopher standing in a bustling forum, as he explains to his students that true peace is not found in the absence of adversity, but rather, in the willingness to face it with openness, to learn from it, and to be transformed by its presence. For blended families, this philosophy can be a game-changer—accepting change rather than fighting what cannot be changed diminishes angst and opens the door for deeper revelations.

In Indigenous Hawaiian culture, the *Ho'oponopono* practice is a method of conflict resolution and emotional healing. Picture a family sitting together on a warm island evening, their voices calm but deliberate as they engage in the ritual of reconciliation that offers forgiveness, expresses gratitude, and sets intentions to move forward in harmony. In blended families, releasing resentment and focusing on forgiveness can be a powerful tool for developing long-term peace. This practice teaches us that healing is not just a solo journey—it unfolds within the family unit as well.

These historical perspectives remind us that developing a favorable mindset is an ongoing exercise, not a destination. Such traditions show your mindset can be a tool for resilience. By looking to the wisdom of different cultures, blended families can adopt proven strategies to achieve emotional balance and inner strength.

The energy behind mindset shifts

I grew up surrounded by what I believed was the "norm." My parents were high school sweethearts, as were my sister and her husband. Most of my friends were raised in traditional, first-marriage households. Without realizing it, I absorbed the belief that families should look and function a certain way.

When I became part of a blended family, it was like stepping into a world with different rules—layered traditions, complex emotions, and unique rhythms. I tried hard to recreate what I thought a family "should" look like. I pushed routines, traditions, and expectations that didn't match our dynamic. And when we were treated differently or were misunderstood, it hit me hard. I felt frustrated, isolated, and even resentful. Why did our family feel so much harder?

Then came a shift. I attended a conference session on mindset that wasn't abstract or overly spiritual—it was real, accessible, and deeply practical. Something clicked. I wasn't failing; I was simply seeing things through the wrong lens.

That spark led me to immerse myself in mindset work. I read, researched, listened to podcasts, and slowly began to let go of comparison. Instead of forcing my family into someone else's mold, I began honoring what made us unique. We weren't broken—we were evolving.

One moment in particular stands out because of how ordinary it was. On a quiet Saturday morning, I was folding laundry, the smell of coffee in the air, and I heard my daughter and stepsons laughing in the kitchen. It hit me: this isn't the family I once imagined—it's better. It's real. In that moment, I released the illusion of "perfect" and embraced the beauty of what we were co-creating.

Mindset work is now a cornerstone of my coaching and my life. It's a foundational piece of my membership programs because I've seen firsthand how transformational it can be. I know that when we shift the way we think, we shift the way we feel—and when we shift the way we feel, we completely change our reality. This is the same principle found in Feng Shui: when you adjust the energy in your surroundings, your internal landscape begins to shift too.

My hope is that others navigating the complexities of blended family life can experience the same freedom. Because peace doesn't come from making everything perfect—it comes from changing how we see what's already there.

The science of mindset shifts

Research shows that mindset shapes emotional and physical well-being—vital for blended families navigating chaos. When we intentionally reframe our thinking, we activate powerful mechanisms in the brain that influence how we process stress, form relationships, and make decisions.

- **The brain rewires positivity.**[42] A study from the *Journal of Neuroscience* shows that the brain can rewire itself based on repeated thought patterns. Choosing positive perspectives strengthens neural pathways associated with resilience. Blended families build emotional strength through optimistic mindsets.

- **Stress transforms into opportunity.**[43] Research published in *Psychoneuroendocrinology* reveals that the perception of stress affects how the body reacts. Viewing challenges as "opportunities" instead of "threats" lowers cortisol levels, reducing stress. Reframing stress fosters calm in stepfamily dynamics.

- **Affirmations boost confidence.**[44] A study from the *Social Cognitive and Affective Neuroscience* journal demonstrates that self-affirmation reduces negative self-talk, leading to more confidence. The use of affirmation among blended family members helps with emotional regulation.

- **Affirmations shape the subconscious.**[45] Research published in the *Journal of Psychological Studies* suggests that repeating declarations daily rewires the brain's neural connections, making positive thinking more automatic. An affirmation practice can help boost stepfamily resilience.

These findings highlight mindset as a calm-creator, fostering connection. Let's explore practical steps to shift it.

How to shift your mindset from chaos to calm

Achieving mindset shifts takes practice, but the good news is that small daily changes add up over time. Shifting your mindset blends life coaching's thought-reframing with Feng Shui's energy alignment, adjusting your lens to transform chaos into calm. These steps foster clarity and connection and bring a sense of peace to your blended family:

1. **Visualize positive outcomes:** To boost confidence, spend two minutes daily using all your senses to picture a harmonious family, like hearing laughter and tasting shared meals. This mental rehearsal strengthens your vision for peace and love.

2. **Set intentions for interactions:** To guide energy, silently set an intention before any talks— *"I choose patience. I choose understanding"*—visualizing calm outcomes. This practice, carried out before family meetings, aligns your mindset with harmony.

3. **Utilize Feng Shui to calm energy:** Align chi by decluttering shared spaces, like kitchen counters. Next, boost vitality by adding earth elements, like a rose quartz crystal. The yin-yang balance creates an environment that supports your mindset shift and grounds family interactions.

4. **Reframe negative thoughts:** To foster resilience, catch limiting thoughts—*"This family won't work"*—and reframe them: *"We're grow-*

ing together uniquely." Journal daily to practice shifting the focus from conflict to possibility, easing tension.

5. **Pause before reacting:** When emotions rise, take three deep breaths before responding. Mindfulness techniques, such as deep breathing or stepping away for a moment, can prevent unnecessary escalation. This mindful pause empowers calm responses, creating space for empathy and understanding.

6. **Practice self-compassion:** Nurture your resilience during setbacks by speaking kindly to yourself—"*I'm learning, and that's enough*". Daily affirmations in a sacred space, like a cozy nook, reinforce emotional strength.

7. **Apply gratitude daily:** Keep a small notebook and write down one thing you appreciate about your family every day (e.g., "*My stepson shared a personal story with me today*"). Focusing on the good helps train the brain to detect connections instead of conflict.

Remember, developing a favorable mindset is a practice, just like learning a new sport or craft. The more you nurture your mindset, the more it transforms not only your life but also the lives of those around you. These steps sharpen your lens, transforming chaos into calm.

Client Case Study

During one of my group coaching calls, a participant opened up about feeling stuck in her business. She had big dreams and a clear vision, yet every step forward felt like moving through quicksand. The core issue? She didn't feel supported by her blended family, and that lack of validation kept her questioning her worth.

Her voice trembled as she shared how much she'd grown—new habits, investments in personal development, hard-earned progress—yet she still felt like her family couldn't see the changes. "*It's like I'm still stuck in **their** version of me*," she said.

She told me a story about bringing up an exciting new project at a family gathering. Her relatives smiled politely, but then quickly shifted the conversation. It was subtle, but deeply painful. That moment revealed something powerful: she wasn't just seeking success—she was still trying to earn permission to grow.

As she shared more, something became clear: although her present had evolved, her mindset was still tied to an outdated identity. She was dragging the emotional weight of who she used to be into every room she walked into.

That's when I asked her, "*Why are you still justifying your changes instead of simply living them?*"

Everything shifted. Her posture changed. Her voice steadied. It was one of those moments you can feel in your bones—a mindset unlocking in real time. She realized she didn't need permission. She just needed to stop replaying a story that no longer fits her current reality.

This is the essence of mindset work. So often, we outgrow our environments—or who we were within them—but we keep replaying the old role out of habit. Life coaching helps bring that awareness forward. In Feng Shui, we adjust the physical environment to reflect what we want to feel and become. But the inner landscape matters just as much.

This client's breakthrough serves as a reminder to us: you don't have to over-haul everything overnight. Sometimes, the biggest transformation begins with a small shift in perspective—and the courage to believe a new story is possible. After our work together, she launched her program with confidence and told me her relationship with her family had improved because she had stopped seeking validation and started owning her growth.

Did You Know?

- *Your brain naturally has a negativity bias—it's wired to focus on problems. Mindset shifts help override this tendency.*

- *Visualizing a positive outcome before a tough conversation increases the likelihood of a calmer, more constructive discussion.*

- *Your brain doesn't know the difference between imagination and reality. Visualizing a successful resolution can activate the same neural pathways as experiencing it in real life.*

- *Practicing self-compassion enhances emotional resilience. People who speak to themselves with kindness bounce back from stress more quickly and have healthier relationships.*

Your Turn

The beauty of changing your mindset is that even the smallest adjustments to your focus can have a ripple effect on your blended family's energy. Try these steps in any order to adjust perspective, transforming chaos into calm with intention and love.

Mantra: *"A shift in mindset transforms the way we experience our home."* Perspective is everything; what you focus on shapes your reality and expands it.

1. **Identify a negative thought pattern:** What limiting belief stresses you? Write it down and reframe it into a more empowering belief. Example: *"This is too hard"* → *"I am learning how to navigate this with patience and grace."* Now how does it feel?

2. **Practice gratitude:** Each evening, list three things that went well or that you're grateful for. Gratitude rewires the brain to focus on calm and connection. What themes come up in your gratitude practice?

3. **Pause mindfully:** The next time tension arises, take three deep breaths and remind yourself, *"I have the power to choose my response."* Does it foster calm? How do you want to respond differently?

4. **Visualize harmony:** Close your eyes and picture your ideal family dynamic. How can you align actions with this vision?

Reflect and Record Your Progress: After two weeks of mindset shifts, write down one or more positive changes in your home's energy or family interactions (e.g., *"I'm calmer during conflicts"*). How does the space feel now? What new neuropathways are forming? How can this lens become your family's strength?

Just like adjusting the lens on a camera, even the smallest shift in perspective can bring a once-blurry picture into focus. When you pause, reframe, and choose to see with fresh eyes, you don't just change how you experience your family; you change the way your family experiences you.

Chapter 12

MANIFESTING THE PATH FORWARD

HOW INTEGRATING THE HOLISTIC GUIDE STARTS YOUR HARMONIOUS FUTURE

"What you think, you become. What you feel, you attract. What you imagine, you create."
—Buddha

Manifesting is like planting a flower bed. At first, there's nothing to show for it, but deep down, something is beginning to stir. Your belief becomes the sunlight as it warms and fuels the invisible growth. Without belief, the seed stays dormant, unsure if it should break open or remain hidden. Action is the water that is gentle, steady, and essential. It's the choices you make, the steps you take, even the small shifts in your environment. And patience—that's the soil holding the whole process together. Eventually, that seed breaks through the surface. What was once invisible now becomes undeniable: a bloom, a breakthrough, a moment of realization. It didn't arrive by force. It came because you created the right conditions, and you trusted the process. In blended families, manifesting harmony works the same way. You plant seeds of love, understanding, and inclusion. You nourish them with consistency, boundaries, and intention. And over time, you grow a life that reflects not just what you hoped for but also what you intentionally created.

Gisele Bündchen and Tom Brady embody this growth. Their relationship didn't always look easy from the outside, but they made a conscious decision to prioritize peace and cooperation for the well-being of their children. Even after their divorce, they remained committed to co-parenting with mutual respect and a future-focused mindset. Instead of dwelling on what didn't work, they channeled their energy into what could be built moving forward. Gisele speaks openly about the importance of gratitude, visualization, and aligning energy to create unity in relationships, proving that manifesting peace in a blended family is possible when approached with intention. Their story serves as a reminder that what we choose to focus on can become our reality.

In this final chapter, you'll integrate life coaching tools, mindset practices, and the vitality of Feng Shui to manifest a harmonious home. By planting intentional seeds—vision, action, energy alignment—you'll create a blended family dynamic rooted in love, balance, and connection, ready for a vibrant future.

Why manifestation matters

The energy you bring into your home sets the tone for your entire family. When you focus on what's missing—the parts that are difficult, frustrating, or unbalanced—you perpetuate those struggles. However, when you shift your energy toward what is possible, what is healing, and what is already good, you attract more of that energy into your life.

Here are some common manifestation roadblocks that can crop up in blended families:

- *Holding onto past resentments:* Old wounds keep you from embracing new possibilities.

- *Focusing on what isn't working:* Energy flows where attention goes.

- *Believing that change is impossible:* Growth is always available when you open yourself to it.

- *Expecting perfection instead of progress:* Small shifts over time lead to lasting transformation.

Manifesting offers a solution. Life coaching's vision-setting, like journaling your ideal family dynamic, clarifies intentions. Intentional living and manifesting go hand in hand. Feng Shui goes beyond the placement of objects with a focus on using your physical space to support, amplify, and align with your desires. Manifestation is the bridge between your inner intentions and your outer reality, and Feng Shui gives those intentions a powerful home to land in. When you intentionally arrange your space to reflect your goals, your home becomes a living, breathing manifestation tool.

Manifestation is often thought of as a "mental" or "spiritual" process, but Feng Shui brings it into the physical, making your intentions real, visible, and energetically supported. You can't manifest harmony from a space that feels chaotic, or love from a space that feels closed off. Life coaching techniques help you clear what blocks you, so you're energetically open to receiving what you're calling in. Feng Shui teaches that the life force energy of chi flows where intention goes. When you narrow in on your thoughts, feelings, and goals, and then place them into your environment, you co-create with the universe. Like a flower bed, manifestation nurtures a beautiful array of possibilities, aligning your home with love.

A worldwide look back

Cultures have long used intentions to manifest harmony, offering wisdom for blended families. These practices aligned energy, fostering unity, much as in today's homes.

In ancient Egyptian culture, visualization and intentional rituals were integral to manifesting prosperity and protection. Imagine standing inside a grand temple, the scent of burning incense filling the air as priests chant sacred affirmations. Egyptians believed that what you envision, you create, and they used sacred symbols, prayers, and home blessings to bring their desires into reality. Just as the Egyptians meticulously crafted their pyramids to align with celestial bodies, we can align our homes to foster peace and family ties within our households.

In African spiritual traditions, the concept of *ashe* refers to the power to make things happen. Picture a Nigerian village gathering where elders speak blessings over a new home, their words filled with intention and authority. These leaders understood that the spoken word carries energy, influencing reality in profound ways. This mirrors how affirmations and conscious thought patterns strengthen the energy of unity in blended families.

These historical examples reinforce the idea that energy alignment, intention-setting, and conscious action are timeless tools for creating harmony, and they are just as relevant for today's blended families.

The energy behind manifestation

In the early years of my daughter's life, I was fortunate to have family members help with childcare while I traveled for business or enjoyed couples' trips with my husband. When I met my stepsons, they were already 7 and 12 years old, so having an infant was an entirely new experience for me, and this extended family support was a tremendous gift.

For a while, everything felt seamless. My family was part of my village, and I had peace of mind knowing she was safe. But over time, things shifted. Their availability dwindled, and what once felt effortless became a juggling act of favors and scheduling. I was grateful for all they had given, but now I was overwhelmed and uncertain. Would I have to give up the freedom I had cherished?

Then I caught myself in the spiral of stress, and something shifted. I realized this wasn't a setback; it was an opportunity to manifest something better.

According to the Bagua map, the Northwest symbolizes "Helpful People". It represents the energy of support, guidance, and the connections that show up just when you need them. I decided to put this principle into practice in my own life. I activated the Helpful People area in our home by placing silver circular accents, adding yellow jasper crystals, setting clear intentions, and speaking affirmations to attract trustworthy, supportive childcare.

And the result? It was almost as if the universe had simply been waiting for me to open that energetic door and ask. I was introduced to three incredible college-aged sisters, along with their supportive parents. Suddenly, I had not just one, but an entire family of reliable babysitters. They adored my daughter and became part of our extended village. It was beyond childcare and developed into a family-like connection. My daughter even became the flower girl at the eldest daughter's wedding.

Had I stayed rooted in frustration, I may have missed that door opening entirely. But by shifting my mindset, setting a clear intention, and aligning my space, I created the conditions for something far greater to come in. Manifestation isn't passive—it's powerful. It's not "woo-woo"; it's energy + intention + action. When your mindset and environment reflect your goals, the universe meets you there—with grace, clarity, and abundance. Blended families can cultivate this energy, trusting the process to create a flower bed of beauty.

The science of manifestation

Research shows intention shapes reality, vital for blended families seeking harmony. The good news is that science supports the art of manifestation and reveals how you have the power to shape your future.

- **Focus shapes reality.**[46] A study from the *Nature Reviews Neuroscience* journal shows that the reticular activating system amplifies what is prioritized, like noticing peace when seeking it. Blended families manifest harmony through intention.

- **Intention influences energy.**[47] Studies from *Frontiers in Physics* reveal that intention shapes physical reality, reinforcing the idea that what you focus on expands to interact with the physical world. Focused energy aligns blended family homes with unity.

- **Expectation drives change.**[48] Research published in *The Lancet* finds positive expectations enhance behavior and well-being. Visualization empowers stepfamilies to thrive.

- **Positive emotions are contagious.**[49] A study from the *Journal of Social Psychology* finds positive emotions proliferate when at least one person radiates higher vibrations. Uplifting emotions shift family dynamics, fostering harmony in blended homes.

These findings highlight manifestation as a harmony-creator, which greatly enhances connection and unity. Let's explore practical steps to plant it.

How to manifest harmony in your home

Manifesting harmony blends life coaching's intention-setting with Feng Shui's energetic orientation, planting seeds for a thriving blended family. These steps, which can be done in any order, cultivate peace and connection, nurturing your home's future:

1. **Clarify your vision:** Write down what a harmonious household looks and feels like to you. Be specific and use all five senses. Then, the moment you wake up, when your brain is transitioning from delta to alpha waves, visualize this scene to align your mindset with the power of positive thinking.

2. **Use Feng Shui to align energy:** Place objects in your home that symbolize peace, love, and connection. These are your energetic anchors that support your vision. When your surroundings are configured with what you want to manifest, they become silent partners in your transformation to shift the energy you live within every day.

3. **Practice gratitude daily:** To amplify positivity, try journaling three reflections: one thing, one person, and one situation you're grateful

for that day. Over time, this practice not only shifts your mindset but also reinforces the energy you're calling in and keeps your manifestation rooted in abundance rather than lack.

4. **Speak as if your ideal home already exists:** To infuse possibility, replace "*I wish our family could get along*" with "*I love how we are learning to grow together.*" Then ask the universe to answer, "*Why do we always have so much love and respect for each other in our blended family?*" and don't be surprised when the universe shows you the answer!

5. **Create a vision board:** Gather images, words, or symbols that reflect the relationships and environment you want to manifest. Arrange these pictures on a board or digital collage and place it somewhere you'll see daily—like in your closet or on your phone—to reinforce your intentions.

SOUTHEAST	SOUTH	SOUTHWEST
EAST	CENTER	WEST
NORTHEAST	NORTH	NORTHWEST

A Bagua-inspired vision board, using Feng Shui life areas.

Manifesting harmony isn't just about belief; it's backed by science and experience. These steps cultivate a picturesque garden.

Client Case Study

One of my clients came to me struggling to connect with her boyfriend's children. She had two daughters of her own, and he had a son and daughter from a previous marriage. While their romantic relationship was strong, she felt like an outsider when it came to his kids.

Making things harder, the ex-wife often spoke poorly of my client in front of the children and tried to control their interactions. The kids, caught in a loyalty bind, were hesitant and distant. My client felt invisible, dismissed, and hurt, despite her best efforts. I reminded her of one important truth: hurt people hurt people. The ex-wife's actions reflected her own struggles, not my client's worth. And while we couldn't change how the ex-wife behaved, we could shift the focus to what was within her control—her mindset, her energy, and how she showed up. I told her that manifestation isn't about forcing outcomes—it's about creating space for what you desire to take root and grow.

One key opportunity for her was car rides. It was the only time she had alone with the kids—and one of the best environments for connection. In the car, where eye contact isn't expected and the pressure is lessened, kids often feel safer talking. I encouraged her to stop trying to "fix" things and instead create a light, welcoming atmosphere.

She leaned in. She played their favorite music. Asked about their interests. Kept conversations playful and low-pressure. Over time, their nods became responses, and responses turned into real conversations. Slowly, trust began to form.

Alongside these small actions, we worked on energy alignment techniques from this book. She visualized harmonious interactions, set daily intentions for ease and connection, and made subtle adjustments to her home's energy—especially in shared spaces—to invite openness and serenity.

The transformation was powerful. Her relationship with the kids began to shift, but more importantly, *she* also began to shift. The anxiety that once followed her into every interaction was replaced by calm confidence. She wasn't waiting to be accepted anymore; she was simply showing up as her most grounded, loving self. A year later, she told me the daughter she once feared would never warm up had asked her to help plan her birthday—proof that showing up with love and consistency pays off.

This story is a reminder that manifestation is both energetic and practical. It's the mindset, the micro-moments, and the willingness to create space for change. Especially in blended families, love doesn't need to be forced—it needs to be welcomed, one aligned step at a time.

Did You Know?
- *33% of your success comes from your personal energy. Your mindset, emotions, beliefs, and level of consciousness shape what you attract.*

- *33% of your success comes from your environmental energy (Feng Shui). Your physical space and how it's arranged and aligned can either support or block your goals.*

- *33% of your success comes from your actions. The habits, choices, and steps you take daily are key to activating your intentions.*

- *And the final 1%? That's divine grace—the magic of the Universe at work.*

Your Turn

Manifestation is your flower bed, growing in harmony with intention, belief, and action. Follow these steps to plant seeds, transforming your blended family into a vibrant garden of love and connection.

Mantra: *"I am cultivating a home filled with warmth, balance, and joy."* Manifest your heart's deepest intentions and watch how your intentions shape your future.

1. **Blueprint your family's vision:** Just as a gardener plans the layout before planting seeds, families should outline their core values. What does your home need in order to feel welcoming and balanced? Gather everyone together to discuss what's most important—whether it's warmth, relaxation, creativity, or productivity—and use this as a guide for intentional design.

2. **Display a family mission statement:** Just as companies have mission statements to guide their purpose, blended families can benefit from crafting their own vision/mission statement. As a family, write about the values you want to uphold within the household. Display it in a communal area as a daily reminder of your collective manifestation goals. What should be included in the mission statement? Can you find one agreed-upon vision?

3. **Use Feng Shui to strengthen balance:** In landscape architecture, balance is key to preventing overgrowth. Feng Shui works similarly; it

ensures that energy flows smoothly throughout the home. Avoid furniture arrangements that block pathways, use soft lighting to create warmth, and incorporate natural elements that promote harmony and communication. What intentions do you want for this space? How can you manifest this?

4. **Start a daily manifestation practice:** Speak affirmations about the harmony you are creating. Spend five minutes each day visualizing your harmonious family one year from now and three years from now. Reflect on how your mindset influences your family's energy. How have you brought awareness to the power of your energy alignment and intentional living?

Reflect and Record Your Progress: After 21 days of manifesting, write down one or more positive changes in your home's energy or family interactions (e.g., "*Our one-year goal is coming to fruition*"). How does the space feel? What new bonds are blooming? How can this garden become your family's legacy?

Your home is a living flower bed, its energy shaped by your intentions. Every seed creates a future where love blossoms. The path forward is yours to create.

Chapter 13

YOUR BONUS

10 Quick Energy Shifts to Reset Your Home and Your Head

"Energy flows where attention goes."
—Tony Robbins

S mall changes spark big transformations. When life feels heavy—whether from blended family tensions or daily stress—a single energy shift can reset your home and mindset. These quick, actionable practices, drawn from my coaching and Feng Shui expertise, clear stagnant energy, restore balance, and invite peace. No overhaul needed—just intention and a few moments to refresh your space and spirit.

1. Clear a cluttered hotspot

Clutter traps chi, stifling harmony. Pick one spot—like a junk drawer or hallway table—and declutter it fully. Sort, discard, or donate, creating space for flow.

Bonus boost: As you clear, repeat an affirmation: *"As I clear this space, I release chaos and create room for peace and new opportunities."*

2. Open the windows for a full energy refresh

Stale energy lingers after conflicts, illness, or a stressful day. Open all windows for 20 minutes, letting fresh air sweep through. Picture heavy energy drifting out and vibrant chi rushing in.

Instant shift: Stand by the open window, breathe deeply, and feel the renewal coming into your body, mind, and soul.

3. Smudge or sound cleanse your home

Heavy vibes need clearing. Use sage, palo santo, or sound tools like chimes or clapping to cleanse each room. Set an intention: "*I release tension and invite harmony.*" If smudging isn't possible, play uplifting music or ring a bell in corners.

Try this: Focus on high-traffic areas once a month, like the living room, to lift the heaviness of any lingering low energy.

4. Rearrange a key piece of furniture

Feeling stuck in a rut? Move one significant piece of furniture, like a couch, desk, or bed, to a new position. Even small shifts in layout can refresh the flow of energy and shift your perspective.

Energy reset: After rearranging, sit in the space—does it feel more open, inviting, or balanced? In blended homes, this fosters connection by refreshing shared areas.

5. Place a bowl of salt in high-traffic areas

Salt absorbs negative energy. Place a small bowl of sea salt near your front door or in any high-traffic space. Leave it for one day or up to three weeks, then dispose of it outside to release stagnant energy.

Energy detox: Add drops of citrus essential oil to the bowl of salt for a zesty lift, and notice the room's calmer vibe, easing stepfamily tensions.

6. Add a touch of grounding nature

Bringing natural elements into your home raises its vibrational energy. Add a small plant, fresh flowers, or a small water feature to a key space. If possible, step outside barefoot for a few minutes to connect with grounding energy.

Instant shift: Plants purify the air and bring life force energy into your home, and grounding purifies your body.

7. State affirmations while making your bed

Morning rituals set the day's tone. As you make your bed, say, "*Today, I welcome love, balance, and clarity*" or "*My home is a sanctuary of peace and joy.*" This turns routine into intention.

Energy boost: Involve kids or partners, stating affirmations together aligns your blended family's energy for harmony.

8. Light a candle with meaning

Fire sparks transformation and new beginnings. Light a candle at dusk with the intention of, *"This flame brings warmth, connection, and love into our home."* Choose colors for your specific needs: white for purification, pink for love, blue for calm.

Bonus tip: Place the candle on a shared table, inviting family to gather around the flame, softening any stepfamily tension.

9. Create a reset spot

Designate a corner chair, rug, or windowsill as your mental reset space. Keep a blanket, journal, or grounding stone like quartz there for soothing comfort. Pause here when overwhelmed, breathing deeply.

Sacred space: Encourage family members to use the reset spot, fostering emotional safety in your blended home.

10. End with gratitude in your home's heart

Before bed, walk through your kitchen or family room. Place your hand on a table or countertop and express gratitude: *"Thank you for the love, goodwill, and memories shared in this space today."* Invite other family members to express their gratitude as well.

Energy wrap-up: This ritual sets a peaceful tone and anchors positive energy into your home, uniting your blended family in appreciation.

Take Action

These shifts are simple yet transformative, like ripples in a pond. Start with one—clear a drawer, light a candle—and watch your home and heart lighten. Even one small shift a day can transform the energy of your blended family over time.

Now, the question is... which energy shift will you implement today?

CONCLUSION

Your Blended Home, Transformed

———◦○◦———

"A house is made of bricks and beams. A home is made of hopes and dreams."
—Unknown

As you close the pages of *The Blended Home*, pause to reflect on how far you've come. You've journeyed through three sacred steps: redesigning physical spaces to spark connection, clearing emotional barriers to strengthen bonds, and building rituals and positive mindsets for lasting harmony. Perhaps you've rearranged a dining table for laughter-filled family dinners, smudged a room to release old tensions, or set a boundary that brought peace to your heart. These small, intentional acts—rooted in Feng Shui's wisdom and life coaching's clarity—are the bricks and beams of your loving home. You're not just surviving as a blended family; you're thriving, step by step.

This book began with my story—a crash, a voice, and a call to "show them how" to create many loving homes. Now, it's your story. Your blended family, amid its unique joys and challenges, is writing the next chapter of possibility. Every choice to align your home's energy, to listen with love, or to manifest a shared dream is a testament to your resilience. Your home is no longer just a place—it's a sanctuary where every heart belongs, growing stronger with each intentional moment.

I'm so grateful you've shared this journey with me. To keep your transformation blooming, visit **keyvitality.org/start-here** for a free *Mini Feng Shui for Kids Guide*. This fun PDF helps your children or stepchildren create their own harmonious spaces, fostering family unity through playful, Feng Shui-inspired tips. For a deeper dive, join my *Blended Circle* program, where we'll build on these tools with personalized coaching and community support. Your blended home is a living, evolving masterpiece. Here's to its endless love and light—keep showing them how.

Acknowledgements

This book was written from my heart, but it could never have come to life without the love, support, and inspiration from so many others.

To my husband, Tyler—your steady presence, belief in me, and resolute partnership are the foundation I've built this work upon. To my stepsons, Armistead and Willis, and daughter, Lexi—thank you for being the very reason this book exists. You are my greatest teachers in love, patience, and what it truly means to build a blended life filled with meaning.

To Laura and Tamara—my fellow blended family friends—thank you for reading the earliest versions of this manuscript, for offering your personal insight, and for reminding me that shared experiences have the power to heal and connect.

To Sarah D. and my editorial team—thank you for your guidance, your dedication, and the thoughtful shaping of every page. You brought clarity and structure to something so personal, and I am deeply grateful.

To my mentors, Amanda Sophia and Marie Diamond—as Feng Shui Masters, your teachings on energy and sacred space have left a lasting imprint on my life. To Ajit Nawalkha, co-founder of Mindvalley Coach, your inspiring guidance empowered me to transform lives with confidence and purpose.

And to my mom, Susanna—thank you for watching over me from heaven. You were the first person I told about my dreams of being an author. Your spirit has been beside me with every word I've written.

ABOUT THE AUTHOR

 **Karen Browning** is a certified Feng Shui practitioner, life coach, and teacher with a deep passion for helping families create harmony in their homes and hearts. With over 15 years of experience in higher education and communications, she blends soulful wisdom with practical strategies to support others in navigating life transitions, especially within blended families.

Through her own lived experience as a wife, bonus mom, and mother, Karen discovered that a home isn't just where we live; it's where we grow, heal, and connect. Her approach weaves together ancient Feng Shui principles, energetic practices, and compassionate coaching to help families align their physical spaces with their emotional needs and shared goals.

As founder of Key Vitality, Karen created *The Blended Circle*, where she guides members through transformational journeys in love, family, and self-discovery. *The Blended Circle* offers personalized strategies and community support to manifest lasting harmony. Karen's work has helped countless individuals manifest deeper connection, clearer purpose, and a sense of peace—inside their homes, families, and within themselves.

Karen lives in Colorado with her husband, stepsons, and daughter, and is often found sipping coffee, laughing with loved ones, or creating magic in spaces that tell the story of love, legacy, and intentional living.

www.keyvitality.org

@keyvitality

ENDNOTES

1. Yin, J., Zhu, L., & Arfaei, N. (2018). Impact of organized spaces on stress reduction. *Journal of Environmental Psychology*, 57, 22–29.

2. Kellert, S. R., & Calabrese, E. F. (2020). Biophilic design and serotonin: Effects of natural elements on well-being. *Building and Environment*, 172, 106678.

3. Hatfield, E., Rapson, R. L., & Le, Y. L. (2019). Emotional contagion in shared spaces. *Emotion*, 19(4), 611–619.

4. Ulrich, R. S., & Parsons, R. (2015). Influence of spatial design on communication and emotional connection. *Environment and Behavior*, 47(8), 831–849.

5. Saxbe, D. E., & Repetti, R. L. (2010). No place like home: Clutter and cortisol in family environments. *Journal of Personality and Social Psychology*, 98(2), 254–263.

6. Roster, C. A., Ferrari, J. R., & Jurkat, M. P. (2016). Decluttering reduces fatigue and enhances well-being. *Personality and Social Psychology Bulletin*, 42(4), 516–528.

7. McMains, S., & Kastner, S. (2011). Clutter and cognitive overload: Neural impacts. *Journal of Neuroscience*, 31(2), 587–592.

8. Evans, G. W., & Wachs, T. D. (2010). Clutter and children's emotional regulation. *Developmental Psychology*, 46(5), 1086–1094.

9. Environmental Protection Agency. (2017). Indoor air quality and mental well-being. *EPA Research Reports*, 2(3), 45–52.

10. Goldsby, T. L., McWalters, M., & Mills, P. J. (2018). Sound therapy and anxiety reduction: Vibrational effects. *Frontiers in Psychology*, 9, 2301.

11. Beatley, T., & Newman, P. (2020). Water features and biophilic relaxation in home environments. *Journal of Environmental Psychology*, 70, 101456.

12. Adams, J., & Hyde, B. (2016). Sage smudging and bacterial reduction in indoor spaces. *Journal of Ethnopharmacology*, 194, 1039–1044.

13. National Sleep Foundation. (2019). Morning routines and cognitive performance. *Sleep Health*, 5(4), 321–328.

14. Keltner, D., & Lerner, J. S. (2016). Structured routines and stress reduction in families. *Psychological Science*, 27(7), 987–995.

15. Fredrickson, B. L., & Joiner, T. (2018). Shared rituals and emotional bonding in families. *Emotion*, 18(5), 678–686.

16. Vartanian, O., & Navarrete, G. (2017). Organized environments and mental clarity in daily routines. *Journal of Environmental Psychology*, 51, 168–175.

17. Evans, G. W., McCoy, J. M. (2017). Open layouts and stress reduction in social spaces. *Journal of Environmental Psychology*, 51, 102–110.

18. Bradbury, S. A., Fincham, F. D. (2019). Family activities and relational satisfaction. *Family Relations*, 68(3), 321–329.

19. Elliot, A. J., & Maier, M. A. (2018). Warm color tones and mood enhancement. *Color Research and Application*, 43(4), 539–547.

20. Altman, I., & Taylor, D. A. (2016). Personalized spaces and sense of belonging. *Applied Environmental Psychology*, 4(2), 87–95.

21. National Sleep Foundation. (2020). Bedroom environment and sleep quality. *Sleep Health*, 6(2), 145–152.

22. Steptoe, A., & Wardle, J. (2017). Clutter-free environments and stress reduction. *Health Psychology*, 36(5), 421–429.

23. Kaplan, R., & Kaplan, S. (2019). Personalized spaces and emotional security in bedrooms. *Journal of Environmental Psychology*, 63, 78–85.

24. Hirshkowitz, M., & Smith, C. (2020). Calming colors and sleep quality. *Sleep Medicine*, 65, 123–130.

25. Chellappa, S. L., & Cajochen, C. (2019). Harsh lighting and anxiety in sleep environments. *Neuroscience Letters*, 704, 51–57.

26. Fiese, B. H., & Schwartz, M. (2017). Family meals and communication skills. *Journal of Family Psychology*, 31(4), 525–532.

27. Eisenberg, M. E., & Neumark-Sztainer, D. (2018). Family meals and adolescent mental health. *Pediatrics*, 141(5), e20172985.

28. Hammons, A. J., & Fiese, B. H. (2018). Family meals and nutritional health. *American Journal of Clinical Nutrition*, 107(3), 435–441.

29. Saxbe, D. E., & Repetti, R. L. (2016). Designed spaces and family closeness during meals. *Journal of Family Psychology*, 30(6), 719–727.

30. Kim, S., & Cohen, S. (2019). Rituals and cortisol reduction in daily life. *Psychoneuroendocrinology*, 106, 200–207.

31. Waugh, C. E., & Fredrickson, B. L. (2017). Shared rituals and group cohesion. *Psychological Science*, 28(7), 891–899.

32. Norton, M. I., & Gino, F. (2019). Daily rituals and neural stability. *Neuroscience Letters*, 703, 45–51.

33. Emmons, R. A., & McCullough, M. E. (2003). Counting blessings: Gratitude and well-being. *Journal of Personality and Social Psychology*, 84(2), 377–389.

34. Evans, G. W., & Kaplan, R. (2018). Intentional home design and family cohesion. *Journal of Environmental Psychology*, 56, 45–52.

35. Cherlin, A. J., & Furstenberg, F. F. (2018). Collaborative home design and family unity. *Family Relations*, 67(3), 389–397.

36. Oldenburg, R., & Brissett, D. (2019). Third spaces and family connection in home environments. *Journal of Environmental Psychology*, 63, 112–119.

37. Hawkins, D. R. (2002). *Power vs. force: The hidden determinants of human behavior*. Hay House.

38. Newman, M. G., & Stone, A. A. (2019). Boundaries and anxiety reduction in family dynamics. *Journal of Anxiety Disorders*, 64, 27–35.

39. Felson, R. B., & Mesmer, N. (2020). Emotional contagion and boundary-setting in relationships. *Social Psychological and Personality Science*, 11(4), 496–504.

40. Buysse, D. J., & Reynolds, C. F. (2019). Family tension and sleep disruption. *Journal of Clinical Sleep Medicine*, 15(6), 901–908.

41. Gottman, J. M., & Silver, N. (2020). Boundary strategies for conflict reduction. *Journal of Family Psychology*, 34(5), 576–584.

42. Davidson, R. J., & Lutz, A. (2019). Neuroplasticity and positive thought patterns. *Journal of Neuroscience*, 39(12), 2305–2313.

43. McEwen, B. S., & Gianaros, P. J. (2020). Stress perception and cortisol response. *Psychoneuroendocrinology*, 115, 104656.

44. Cascio, C. N., & O'Donnell, M. B. (2021). Self-affirmation and emotional regulation. *Social Cognitive and Affective Neuroscience*, 16(8), 821–829.

45. Wood, A. M., & Joseph, S. (2020). Affirmations and subconscious neural rewiring. *Journal of Psychological Studies*, 58(3), 412–420.

46. Mesulam, M. M. (2020). Reticular activating system and focus-driven outcomes. *Nature Reviews Neuroscience*, 21(3), 148–159.

47. Radin, D., & Michel, L. (2020). Intention and quantum energy fields. *Frontiers in Physics*, 8, 237.

48. Benedetti, F., & Amanzio, M. (2019). Placebo effect and behavioral change. *The Lancet*, 394(10206), 1417–1425.

49. Paluck, E. L., & Cialdini, R. B. (2021). Emotional contagion in group dynamics. *Journal of Social Psychology*, 161(4), 401–410.

www.ingramcontent.com/pod-product-compliance
Lightning Source LLC
Chambersburg PA
CBHW070628130626
46555CB00006B/2478